# J. K. LASSER'S ALL YOU SHOULD KNOW ABOUT IRA, KEOGH, AND OTHER RETIREMENT PLANS

By the J.K. Lasser Tax Institute

Bernard Greisman,
Editor

REVISED AND UPDATED FOR 1986

Published by
Simon & Schuster, Inc., New York

Copyright © 1983, 1984, 1985, 1986 by Simon & Schuster, Inc.

All rights reserved
including the right of reproduction
in whole or in part in any form
Published by Simon & Schuster, Inc.
Simon & Schuster Building
Rockefeller Center
1230 Avenue of the Americas
New York, New York 10020
Simon & Schuster, Inc.

Designed by Irving Perkins Associates

Manufactured in the United States of America

10 9 8 7 6 5 4 3 2 1

Library of Congress Cataloging in Publication Data

ISBN: 0-671-60288-8

West Hills College Coalinga
Fitch Library
300 Cherry Lane
Coalinga, CA 93210

PREFACE

THE tax laws offer incentives to save for retirement by providing benefits to individuals and businesses when they set aside money in pension plans. Whether you are an employer, employee, or are self-employed, J. K. Lasser's *All You Should Know About IRA, Keogh, and Other Retirement Plans* details options for retirement investments and shows you how to take advantage of the tax breaks allowed by law.

To live comfortably during your retirement years, you must start planning early to build up adequate financial resources. Try to choose the type of funding which you can afford and which will meet your goals. This book defines your pension alternatives and examines planning techniques which will yield the maximum tax benefits. You will find expert discussions on what you need to know about reviewing retirement investment choices; setting up an IRA or Keogh plan; establishing an SEP for your small business or using corporate retirement plans; deciding when and how to take distributions from your plan for maximum benefits; avoiding IRA and Keogh tax penalties; keeping records for your retirement investments; your Social Security benefits; and estate planning for your retirement.

This edition reflects the tax law changes proposed for 1986. Congress has complicated retirement planning with frequent changes of tax rules over the last five years. In 1986, Congress may continue this pattern by making several additional radical changes that are discussed in the last chapter of this guide.

This guide will help you make informed decisions about how, when and where to save for a secure retirement.

We gratefully acknowledge the contribution of Elliott Eiss, member of the New York Bar, in the preparation of this book.

Bernard Greisman

CONTENTS

1. INVESTMENT PLANNING FOR RETIREMENT FUNDS   11

Investing in savings institutions, 15   Disadvantages of banking institutions, 18   Investing in annuities offered by insurance companies, 18   Disadvantages of annuities, 20   Setting up an account with a broker, 21   Disadvantages of an account with a broker, 25   Investing in mutual funds, 26   Types of funds, 27   Disadvantages of investing in a mutual fund, 28   Which fund is for you?, 28   Diversifying your investments, 29

2. YOUR IRA   32

What is an individual retirement account?, 32   What is an individual retirement annuity?, 33   IRA break-even point for younger workers, 33   Contributing to a company plan, 35   Figuring your contribution, 37   Age limit on contributions, 38   When to make contributions, 38   IRAs for married couples, 39   IRAs for divorced persons, 41   How distributions are taxed, 41   Reporting requirements for IRAs, 42   Bank penalties on closing time-deposit accounts before maturity, 43   Avoiding excess contribution penalties, 44   Premature distributions may be subject to penalty, 45   How much must you withdraw at age 70½?, 46   Recordkeeping for your IRA, 47

3. YOUR SELF-EMPLOYMENT RETIREMENT PLAN   49

Are you eligible to start a Keogh plan?, 50   Choosing a plan, 51   Choosing the funding structure for your Keogh plan, 152   Defined-contribution limitations, 52   Defined-benefit contribution limitations, 53   When to make annual contributions, 54   Including employees in your plan, 54   Voluntary contributions may allow for increased tax-free accumulations, 55   When can you receive retirement benefits?, 55   Incidental life insurance coverage, 57   How benefits are taxed, 57   U.S. retirement bonds, 58   Penalties, 59   How to qualify your plan, 61   Deducting costs of a plan, 61   Eliminating restrictions on plans for owner-employees, 61

4. YOUR CORPORATE RETIREMENT PLAN 63

Setting up a qualified company retirement plan, 63 Should you start a pension or profit-sharing plan?, 64 Overall limits on retirement contributions and benefits, 67 Covering employees, 70 Integrating a pension or profit-sharing plan with Social Security, 71 When employee benefits must vest, 72 Benefits after 1983 under top-heavy plans, 74 How much is deductible?, 76 When deductions are claimed, 78 When benefits are paid, 78 How benefits from qualified company plans are taxed, 81 Obtaining plan approval, 82 What happens to benefits when an employee terminates employment?, 82 Contributions to S corporation plans, 83 Substantial loans from company plans may be taxed, 83 Reporting requirements, 84

5. SIMPLIFIED EMPLOYEE PENSION PLANS (SEPs) 85

How SEPs compare with other plans, 86 Limits on SEP contributions, 87 If your employer has an SEP, 89 How SEP benefits are taxed, 90 Reporting rules, 90

6. DEFERRED PAY PLANS FOR INCREASED RETIREMENT BENEFITS 91

Should you take a salary reduction?, 92 Cash or deferred-pay plan may not discriminate, 93 Salary-reduction plans for employees of tax-exempt groups and schools, 95

7. TAX TREATMENT OF RETIREMENT BENEFITS 98

How to treat lump-sum distributions from qualified retirement plans, 98 Ten-year averaging, 100 Separation-from-service test for employees, 104 Lump-sum payments received by deceased employee's beneficiary, 105 Securities received as distribution, 106 Rollover of partial distributions, 108 How annuity payments are taxed, 109 Three-year recovery of cost, 110 How annuities are taxed if you cannot use the three-year rule, 111 How Civil Service retirement pay is taxed, 114 How beneficiaries of deceased employees report annuity payments, 116 Military personnel allowed tax exclusion on annuity election, 117 Are your retirement benefits protected from the claims of creditors and ex-spouses?, 118 Withholding tax on pension benefits, 119

8. RETIREMENT BENEFIT OPTIONS AND ROLLOVERS   121

Are your employee benefits vested?, 121   When to take retirement benefits, 122   How to take retirement benefits, 124   Is a rollover advisable when you retire?, 125   Rules for making a tax-free rollover into an IRA or a qualified plan, 125   Changing a rollover election, 128   Rollover of proceeds from sale of property received in lump-sum distribution, 128   Rollovers of IRAs, 129   Tax-free transfer of an IRA because of divorce, 130

9. SOCIAL SECURITY   131

Qualifying for benefits, 131   Applying for Social Security retirement benefits, 134   Payment of benefits, 134   Estimating retirement benefits, 135   Social Security and retirement planning, 136   How Social Security benefits are taxed, 137   Medicare coverage, 138   Filing claims, 141   What Medicare does not cover, 141   Medicare and additional health insurance, 141

10. ESTATE TAX ON RETIREMENT BENEFITS   143

How benefits from qualified plans are taxed, 143   Individual retirement plans (IRAs), 144   How death benefits under nonqualified plans are taxed, 145   Treatment of special retirement benefits, 146

11. GUIDE TO TAX LAW PROPOSALS   148

Chapter 1
INVESTMENT PLANNING FOR RETIREMENT FUNDS

AMERICANS can no longer be complacent about retirement security for two good reasons. We are living longer, perhaps 20 years or more beyond age 65, and for many, Social Security is and will continue to be an inadequate basis of support. Therefore, advance planning is necessary to guarantee a secure retirement.

Fortunately, the tax laws are designed to encourage retirement savings. Tax-approved personal retirement plans offer two main advantages: You can accumulate large funds for retirement without tax erosion and enjoy the immediate benefit of deducting contributions. For example, if you set up an IRA at age 30 and contribute the maximum amount allowed each year until age 65, you will have accumulated more than half a million dollars if your money earns 10% compounded annually, $866,340 at 12%, or $1.7 million at 15%. Also, you will have saved a considerable amount of income taxes: $24,500 if you are in the 35% income tax bracket. The following charts show how much can be accumulated, depending on your contributions and interest rates.

The compounding of interest which accumulates tax free may make it possible for many Americans to become millionaires by undertaking a long-term retirement savings program. The earlier you start your savings program, the more you will have. You might ask, "What will a million dollars be worth 30 or 40 years from now?" No one can say with any certainty, but you may be sure that you will be better off with it than without it.

The major decisions in setting up a retirement account are how and where to invest your savings. Most investments, ranging from savings certificates to real estate, are open to you.

HOW TAX-FREE ANNUAL COMPOUNDING BUILDS UP YOUR RETIREMENT FUND

$2,000 invested annually at

	Number of years invested						
	5	10	15	20	25	30	35	40
8%	$11,740	$28,980	$54,300	$91,520	$146,200	$226,580	$344,640	$518,020
10%	12,200	31,880	63,540	114,540	196,700	328,980	542,040	885,180
12%	12,700	35,100	74,560	144,100	266,660	482,660	866,340	1,534,160
15%	13,480	40,600	95,160	204,880	425,580	869,480	1,762,340	3,558,020

$4,000 invested annually at

	Number of years invested						
	5	10	15	20	25	30	35	40
8%	$23,480	$57,960	$108,600	$183,040	$292,400	$453,120	$689,280	$1,036,040
10%	24,400	63,760	127,080	229,080	393,400	657,960	1,084,080	1,770,360
12%	25,400	70,200	149,120	288,200	533,320	965,320	1,732,680	3,068,320
15%	26,960	81,200	190,320	409,760	851,160	1,738,960	3,524,680	7,116,040

$10,000 invested annually at

	Number of years invested						
	5	10	15	20	25	30	35	40
8%	$58,700	$144,900	$271,500	$457,600	$731,000	$1,132,900	$1,723,200	$2,590,100
10%	61,000	159,400	317,700	572,700	983,500	1,664,900	2,710,200	4,425,900
12%	63,500	175,500	372,800	720,500	1,333,300	2,413,300	4,331,700	7,670,800
15%	67,400	203,000	475,800	1,024,400	2,127,900	4,347,400	8,811,700	17,790,100

$15,000 invested annually at

	Number of years invested						
	5	10	15	20	25	30	35	40
8%	$88,050	$217,350	$407,250	$686,400	$1,096,500	$1,699,350	$2,584,800	$3,885,150
10%	91,500	239,100	476,550	859,050	1,475,250	2,467,350	4,065,300	6,638,850
12%	95,250	263,250	550,200	1,080,750	1,999,950	3,619,950	6,497,550	11,506,200
15%	101,100	304,500	713,700	1,536,600	3,191,850	6,521,100	13,217,550	26,685,150

YOUR TAX SAVING FROM RETIREMENT PLAN CONTRIBUTIONS

	Tax saving from annual $2,000 contribution							
Tax bracket	5	10	15	20	25	30	35	40
15%	$1,500	$3,000	$4,500	$6,000	$7,500	$9,000	$10,500	$12,000
25%	2,500	5,000	7,500	10,000	12,500	15,000	17,500	20,000
35%	3,500	7,000	10,500	14,000	17,500	21,000	24,500	28,000

	Tax saving from annual $4,000 contribution							
Tax bracket	5	10	15	20	25	30	35	40
15%	$3,000	$6,000	$9,000	$12,000	$15,000	$18,000	$21,000	$24,000
25%	5,000	10,000	15,000	20,000	25,000	30,000	35,000	40,000
35%	7,000	14,000	21,000	28,000	35,000	42,000	49,000	56,000

Tax saving from annual $10,000 contribution

Tax bracket	5	10	15	20	25	30	35	40
15%	$7,500	$15,000	$22,500	$30,000	$37,500	$45,000	$52,500	$60,000
25%	12,500	25,000	37,500	50,000	62,500	75,000	87,500	100,000
35%	17,500	35,000	52,500	70,000	87,500	105,000	122,500	140,000

Tax saving from annual $15,000 contribution

Tax bracket	5	10	15	20	25	30	35	40
15%	$11,250	$22,500	$33,750	$45,000	$56,250	$67,500	$78,750	$90,000
25%	18,750	37,500	56,250	75,000	93,750	112,500	131,250	150,000
35%	26,250	52,500	78,750	105,000	131,250	157,500	183,750	210,000

However, yields, risks, and costs vary. Before you decide on an investment, consider the following facts:

1. How does an account fit into your retirement plans? Will it be the only source of funds, in addition to Social Security benefits, or do you have another pension plan? If you can count on other funds for retirement years, you may be willing to take greater risk with your investments. If the retirement account must provide most of your income during retirement, you should follow a more conservative path.

2. How many years do you have until retirement? If retirement is only a few years away, you may seek low-risk, income-oriented investments. Younger persons may be willing to accept higher risk or look for long-term growth.

3. How much risk can you comfortably tolerate? Your investment choice should not keep you awake at night. Only you can decide which investment suits your temperament. If you want to avoid risk as much as possible, invest in insured bank deposits or government securities.

Investing in savings institutions

Banks and savings and loan associations (S&Ls) have been aggressive competitors for retirement account dollars. Since IRAs were first introduced in 1977, banking institutions have attracted the overwhelming number of accounts. Almost 50% of all IRA funds are in savings institutions.

There are several good reasons for this popularity. Banks and S&Ls are conveniently located, familiar institutions. Bank officers are known to customers and can be questioned in person. Retirement accounts at savings institutions enjoy a high measure of safety. Accounts are insured by the FDIC or FSLIC for up to $100,000 in each bank; credit union accounts enjoy similar protection. There are usually no fees for opening or maintaining an account. Banking institutions may pay market rates, as well as enhance returns through interest compounding, and guarantee that return for a fixed term.

Today the banking industry is in the midst of deregulation.

INVESTMENT PLANNING FOR RETIREMENT FUNDS

What this means to the retirement investor is an ever-increasing assortment of savings instruments from which to choose: fixed rate to variable rate; terms from a few days to several years; daily, monthly, or annual compounding and various minimum deposit requirements. Consider the present array of investment options found at savings institutions, such as money market funds and certificates of deposit (CDs) with different maturities and terms.

Bank money market funds are competitive with money market mutual funds. The bank money market funds guarantee for one-week or one-month periods interest rates tied to the Treasury bill rate or the average money market rate. Bank funds also offer this added attraction: They are federally insured. Bank money market accounts require an average monthly balance of $2,500, which the government is planning to phase out; if the account falls below the minimum, interest is reduced.

Investments in money market funds allow you to take advantage of volatile interest rates which are rising. Investments in CDs allow you to lock into the highest available interest rate for a fixed period of time if you are concerned with a decline of rates during that period.

Banking regulations allow banks and savings institutions to pay what they please on certificates of deposit and do not require minimum balances on CDs with terms over 31 days.

Withdrawals within certain limits may be made from money market funds without penalty. Premature withdrawals from CDs are penalized. For certificates with maturities of one year or less, the penalty is a loss of interest of one month; for certificates maturing in more than one year, the penalty is a loss of interest for three months. Banks are free to waive premature withdrawal penalties for those age 59½ and over. If you are over 59½ and you know your bank has traditionally waived the penalty, perhaps you should choose the highest yielding CD, regardless of its term. If you find yourself in a long-term CD when rates rise, you can switch without penalty. Be aware, however, that banks do not have to waive the penalty, or even permit early withdrawals without penalties.

Disadvantages of banking institutions

CD investments in savings institutions allow you to lock into high interest rates only for the short term, generally up to five years. If you are concerned that rates will substantially decline in the future, you may want to invest in a currently available investment that fixes a high rate over longer periods, such as bonds with long-term maturities. Bond investments are discussed later in this chapter.

Banking rules change frequently. Investment options vary from bank to bank. Not all banks offer the maximum rates or compound interest in the same manner. Whether interest is compounded daily or annually may mean a difference of more or less interest depending on the method of computation. Each bank also has its own policy of treating matured certificates. Some banks automatically renew the CD for another term at the current rate unless notified to the contrary; some banks will not renew a matured CD without express authority from you. If you fail to act, you may find your funds switched to a day-of-deposit account on maturity. Banking institutions can also change their rules after you have opened an account. For instance, they may have traditionally waived premature withdrawal penalties for those age 59½ or over, but without announcement, they can reverse this practice.

Investing in annuities offered by insurance companies

Insurance companies have long been in the business of selling annuities. Since the expansion of personal retirement plans, insurance companies have tailored their annuities to accept retirement plan contributions. An annuity is a contract that provides a guaranteed monthly income for life or for a term of years. For every $1,000 invested, you will receive a certain amount each month after retiring. The amount you receive monthly depends on your life expectancy and on the return the company was able to earn on your investments.

The chief advantage of an annuity is the assurance that you can never outlive your capital. You are guaranteed a retirement income for your life or, if you choose, for the lives of you and your spouse. Further, you have complete freedom from investment management. The insurance company invests your contributions as it sees fit, although you may choose from certain types of investments, as discussed later.

Insurance company annuities offer another advantage in this age of mobility: continuity of investment if you move from your current location. Many insurance companies have offices nationwide and can continue to service your account. Even in the absence of a convenient office, you may take your contract with you anywhere and continue to pay premiums by mail.

Types of annuities and contract options. There are two general types of annuities: fixed rate and variable rate. With a fixed-rate annuity, you are guaranteed two rates: a maximum rate guaranteed only for the first year (in some cases two years) of the contract and a minimum rate guaranteed for the term of the contract. The maximum rate offered today approximates the return of a money market fund or one-year Treasury notes. In an insurance company brochure you may find a projection of earnings over the life of the contract based entirely on this high rate. Such a projection may be misleading since the high return is not guaranteed. The minimum return guaranteed by most companies today is low—4% to 6%.

The variable or flexible annuity offers no guaranteed rate. Your return varies with the type of investment. Generally, you may choose to have the insurance company invest in a stock fund, a money market fund, or a fixed-income fund with a guaranteed return which is adjusted periodically. There may be some opportunity to switch among the funds.

With either type of annuity you insure income until you die or until both you and your spouse die. The latter is called a "joint and survivor contract"; payments are actuarially reduced since they will be extended over the lives of both spouses.

An endowment policy may be used as a retirement plan. It provides for the payment of a definite sum after a stated number of years.

A feature unique to insurance company annuities is a disability rider. If you become disabled before your contract has been completed, the company will pay your premiums and continue your retirement account. Thus you receive the same retirement income as if you had not become disabled. Of course, you cannot claim a tax deduction for the insurance company's payment on behalf of your annuity.

Annuities tailored to retirement plans are required to contain certain features. An IRA annuity contract may not require premiums exceeding $2,000. Any refund of premium or dividends must be applied toward the payment of the following year's premiums or toward the purchase of additional benefits. IRA annuity premiums must be "flexible," that is, the contract may not call for a fixed premium but must permit a fluctuating premium. The company may set a minimum annual premium, such as $500, below which they will not write a policy. The contract may not contain any loan provisions. Read the contract carefully. You have seven days from the day you receive the disclosure statement to change your mind without incurring a penalty.

Disadvantages of annuities

A major drawback of investing in annuities is their fees, which are generally classified as "front load" or "back load." In a "front load" annuity, there is an initial charge which is subtracted from every $1,000 invested. One company charges almost $90 per $1,000. Thus of a $2,000 contribution, $180 will go directly to the insurance company and $1,820 will be invested for your benefit. In addition to the initial fee, there may be a small annual maintenance fee. However, if the fees are separately billed and separately paid, they do not reduce the IRA contribution and are currently deductible as an investment expense.

In a "back load" annuity there is no initial fee, but annual maintenance charges beginning in the second year may be substantial—$25 or $30. The company may charge a penalty for early withdrawals from back-load annuities. The penalty, 7% or 8%, decreases each year so that there is no penalty after a certain year, such as the 8th, 10th, or 11th year. One company permits withdrawals of up to 10% of the fund before it imposes penalties. There may also be a small service charge for each withdrawal.

A second major disadvantage of insurance company annuities has been their poor investment return. High returns are not guaranteed beyond the first year or two. In the past, annuities have generally realized a low return compared to other investments.

Another drawback is the lack of legacy resulting from an annuity. If you die ten years or more after your annuity starts and did not select a joint and survivor annuity, your heirs receive nothing.

Finally, be aware that annuities are purchased through insurance agents who earn commissions on the sale of policies. Do not be pressured into a purchase which may not suit your needs.

Setting up an account with a broker

You may open a retirement account at a brokerage firm and choose either a self-directed account or a mutual fund operated by the firm. The main advantage of either type of account is flexibility. With a mutual fund you can share in a managed portfolio of investments, and within a mutual fund family you may switch among funds. In a self-directed account you choose how you wish to invest your money. Most investments, including stocks, bonds, real estate, and oil and gas, are open to you; you may switch or combine your holdings. Some brokerage firms also offer annuities similar to those offered by life insurance companies.

There is no one "right" investment for your retirement account. If you decide to open a self-directed account, you may design a plan to meet your needs and follow investments you think will succeed. Overseeing a personalized plan may be enjoyable, but it requires more effort than other options.

To fund your account, you should consider investments in light of your objectives, preferences, and tolerance for risk. You should also consider the past and present performance of various investments. A study by Roger G. Ibbotson of the University of Chicago's Graduate School of Business and by Rex A. Sinquefield of the American National Bank & Trust Company of Chicago compared selected investments from 1926 through 1978. Common stocks (as indicated by Standard & Poor's 500

Stock Index) led the group with an average annual return of 9%, more than twice the annual return of corporate bonds and Treasury obligations during that period. Inflation in those years averaged 2.5% annually. However, stocks are generally adversely affected by periods of high inflation and have not fared as well recently.

In the measure of average annual returns for the past ten years, bonds placed last with a return of 3.6%. Stocks were only slightly higher, with a 3.9% return. Of course, you should consider the performance of stocks of individual companies and current economic conditions.

For investment purposes, a bond may be described according to the length of the period of maturity. Short-term bonds usually mature within one to five years; medium-term bonds in five to 20 years; long-term bonds in 20 or more years. Where the interest is paid out on a regular schedule, the bond is called a "current income" bond. An accrual or discount bond is a bond on which interest is accumulated and paid as part of the specified maturity value (the bond having been issued at a price lower than the specified maturity value).

The investment value of bonds is generally expressed in rates of yield. There are four types of yield: The nominal or coupon yield; the actual yield; the current market yield; and the net yield to maturity. The nominal or coupon yield is the fixed or contractual rate of interest stated on the bond. A bond paying 11% has a nominal yield of 11%. The actual yield is the rate of return based on the price at which the bond was purchased. If bought below par, the actual yield will exceed the nominal or coupon yield. If bought at a premium (above par) the actual yield will be less than the coupon or nominal yield. For example, if you paid $800 for a $1,000 bond paying 10% interest, the actual yield is 12½% ($100 divided by $800). The current market yield is the rate of return on the bond if bought at prevailing market price. It is figured in the same manner as actual yield. For example, if the 10% bond was quoted at $750, its current yield would be 13⅓%. Net yield to maturity represents the rate of return on the bond if it is held to maturity, plus appreciation allocated to a discount purchase or less reductions for any premium paid on a bond selling above par. If you buy a bond below par at a market discount, your annual

INVESTMENT PLANNING FOR RETIREMENT FUNDS 23

return is proportionately increased by a part of the discount allocated to the number of years before maturity. If the discount was $50 on a bond having a five-year maturity, then your annual income return on the bond is increased by $10 ($50 divided by 5). On the other hand, if you bought at a premium, the extra cost is a reduction against your income because you paid more than can be recovered at maturity. This cost is allocated over the remaining life of the bond. Thus, if you bought a five-year bond at $50 over par, your average annual return is reduced by $10 ($50 divided by 5).

Investment return on a bond is generally limited to the stated interest. You cannot expect any appreciation of principal as you can in a stock investment, unless you have bought bonds selling at a discount.

Daily bond sales and prices on the major exchanges are listed in the major financial dailies. Bond prices fluctuate in response to the changes in interest rates and business conditions. In setting the daily price of a bond, the market weighs the current status, performance, and future prospects of the issuing corporation, as well as the interest rate and maturity period of the bond.

Quotations are based on 100 as equal to par, even though the basic unit for an actual bond may be in denominations of $1,000. A quote of 90½ simply means a bond with a face value of $1,000 will cost $905 at market.

Current interest rates affect the selling price of bonds. If current interest rates increase over the interest rate of your bond, the market value of a bond will decline. The decline in value has nothing to do with the credit rating of the issue. It simply means that other investors will buy only at terms that will give them the current higher return. If you bought a bond paying a rate of 8% at par, $1,000, and a few months later, interest rates go to 11%, another investor will not pay $1,000 for the bond for an 8% return. To match the 11% return on a dollar, the market value of the bond will drop to a level which will return 11% on the money invested, based on its actual 8% return and the period remaining before maturity. Thus, during periods of rising interest, the price of bonds issued at lower rates in prior years declines. This occurs to even top quality bonds; the highest credit rating will not protect the market value of a low-interest-paying bond. When this happens there may be bond bargains available, as prices on outstanding bonds decrease. Bonds bought at deep discounts will yield a profit if held to maturity. The profit is the difference between what you pay and the par value received at maturity. The profit is not taxable if held for qualified retirement plan purposes. If interest rates decline below the interest rate of your bond, the value of your bond will increase, but, at the same time, the company, if it has an exercisable call option, may redeem the bond to rid itself of the high interest cost and attempt to raise funds at current lower rates. Thus, an early redemption of the bond could upset your long-range investment plans in that particular issue.

Investments are designed to take advantage of the retirement account market. For example, zero-coupon bonds are corporate bonds that may be suited to retirement accounts. They are sold at a deep discount from face value and pay no periodic interest. The yield is the difference between the price paid and the face value received at redemption.

An advantage of zero-coupon bonds is that your return is known in advance. However, the value of the bonds fluctuates with interest rate changes so that if you sell before maturity at a time of increasing interest rates, you could lose part of your investment. Zero-coupon bonds are not insured. Seek bonds of reliable companies or zero-coupon Treasury bonds marketed by certain brokerages under such names as "LIONS, TIGRS, and CATS." These zeros are regular Treasury bonds from which the interest coupons have been stripped. The U.S. Government also offers its own version under the name "STRIPS." STRIPS are considered the safest zeros because they are a direct obligation of the U.S. government, but they yield up to one tenth of one percent less than zeros issued by brokerage houses or banks.

Another investment variation designed for retirement accounts is limited partnerships which invest in oil and gas and real estate. These investments are speculative and designed for those willing to gamble a part of their retirement savings. Consider only investments offered through established firms and organized by companies with experience in the field. If you are not familiar with the operations of a partnership, have your financial advisor examine the prospectus.

INVESTMENT PLANNING FOR RETIREMENT FUNDS 25

Disadvantages of an account with a broker

Cost is the major disadvantage of establishing an account with a broker. If you invest in a brokerage mutual fund program, you can expect to pay a setup cost of $15 to $20 and an annual fee of about $20. If you switch among funds, you pay a fee of about $5 for each transaction. A self-directed account is more expensive, with setup fees running $25 to $30 and annual maintenance fees of $35 to $50 or a percentage of your portfolio, such as $2/10$ of 1%. If these fees are separately billed and separately paid, they are currently deductible. In addition to these fees, you pay the broker's commission for buying and selling securities. Some brokers charge more if the account holds a particular kind of investment; some may charge termination fees if you decide to move your account.

Note that investing in securities is more practical when you have saved a few thousand dollars. Some investment advisors suggest that self-directed plans be postponed for the first few years until a fund can be built up. Otherwise, if you plan to buy stocks you will be forced to buy in odd lots or buy lower priced stock, and much of your investment will be eaten up by commissions.

When you invest with a brokerage firm, there is no certainty of investment return or yield. Rates and earnings are not fixed.

Check to see if an account is protected by the Securities Investors Protection Corporation (SIPC). Coverage extends to $500,000 for securities and to $100,000 for cash held in a protected account. SIPC insurance guards only against insolvency of the firm or mismanagement of your account. There is no guarantee against ordinary market losses.

Finally, carefully review the terms of the agreement with your broker. One investor, who put his IRA in a brokerage account, was not allowed by the trustee to transfer from one account to another. Further, the trustee reserved some of the IRA funds to cover broker fees and other transfer costs. The investor asked the IRS if these restrictions violated the tax law. The IRS, in a private letter ruling, said there was no violation. An IRA is a contractual agreement between the IRA trustee and the participant. Although the tax laws do not place limitations on direct IRA-to-IRA transfers, the trustees of a particular account may restrict such transfers.

Investing in mutual funds

Mutual funds have traditionally offered the small investor a way to invest in the market with low minimum requirements. By pooling the money of many individuals, funds enable each investor to share in a large, diversified portfolio and spread the market risks.

In addition to small minimums and good returns, mutual funds offer professional management and a high degree of liquidity. While the funds' professional management is not a guarantee of success, it means that the individual investor does not have to study the market. The liquidity offered by the funds assures easy deposits and withdrawals and no penalties. In fact, money market funds are often used by institutional investors and individuals as a temporary parking place for cash that will later be invested in another instrument.

There are two types of mutual funds: open end and closed end. In an open-end fund, investment companies offer shares to the public continuously. The price of a share is determined by the value of a fund's portfolio, plus other assets and minus liabilities. This figure, divided by the number of shares owned by shareholders, is the fund's net asset value per share, or price. Note that money market funds are an exception; their price usually remains constant at $1 per share. An open-end company will repurchase shares on demand at the prevailing value per share.

A closed-end fund issues a limited number of shares which are traded on stock exchanges. These funds are not obligated to repurchase shares. Prices or net asset values per share (abbreviated NAV) for open-end and closed-end funds can be found in the financial pages of major newspapers. The following discussion is limited to the more common open-end mutual funds.

A mutual fund offers flexibility at low cost. Funds that are "no loads" do not carry any sales charges. Setup fees and transfer fees may be small or nonexistent, and annual maintenance fees may total only $5 or $10. You may incur a small charge if you terminate an account. "Load" funds are sold through brokers or salespersons, and you pay a commission of 6% to 8½%. Fees are paid separately and do not reduce your investment.

A fund may purchase stocks, corporate bonds, money market instruments, government securities, and international investments; it may emphasize growth or income, or aim for both. A fund family is a group of funds managed by the same company. The advantage of a family is that you can easily move your money among the different funds as economic conditions change.

Types of funds

Money market funds—also called liquid asset or cash funds, invest in high-yield money market instruments such as U.S. government securities, bank certificates of deposit, and commercial paper.

Stock funds—invest mainly in equities; they may purchase common and/or preferred stock. Some may concentrate on a particular industry or on companies in a particular area.

Corporate bond funds—invest mainly in company bonds. These funds usually emphasize income rather than growth.

Municipal bond funds—invest in tax-exempt bonds of cities, states, and other local governments.

Aggressive growth funds—emphasize growth or capital appreciation and accept greater risk to achieve it. For example, an aggressive growth fund may borrow money to leverage its investments or use options.

Growth funds—seek long-term capital growth. These funds usually invest in common stocks that have growth potential.

Income funds—try to provide immediate income from dividends and interest instead of long-term growth.

Growth and income funds—aim for both capital appreciation and current income.

Balanced funds—invest in a balance of common stocks and fixed-income instruments, such as preferred stocks and corporate bonds. With their conservative investment policy, the value of these funds generally does not fluctuate as widely as the market.

Option income funds—invest in dividend-paying common stocks on which call options are traded on the major exchanges.

These funds accept the risks involved in options to provide high income.

Disadvantages of investing in a mutual fund

Using mutual funds for your retirement account has drawbacks, primarily a lack of assured return and the absence of insurance. The return fluctuates with market conditions. In the past few years money market funds have had high annual returns, but there is no assurance that such yields will continue. The best way to assess the reliability of a particular fund is to check its record over the past several years. Three investment services that publish this information are: United Business Service, Weisenberger Investment Companies Source, and Lipper Analytical Services.

There is also the following problem: IRA investors in funds have encountered delays in being able to transfer their accounts from one fund to another. Some delays have been up to six months and have prevented investors from taking advantage of market changes. Stock exchange authorities have been pressing funds and brokers to complete transfers within 10 days, but there is no guarantee that a fund will be able to meet this request.

Which fund is for you?

If you do opt for mutual funds, the experts recommend that you diversify into different types of funds within a mutual fund family. For example, you could use both a money market fund and a stock fund.

Some tax authorities advise against stock funds for retirement accounts for two reasons: losses are not deductible; and earnings that would normally be taxed at favorable capital gain rates are considered ordinary income when withdrawn from the IRA. Other authorities, however, suggest that stock funds emphasizing growth may be ideal for younger workers who can wait out the short-term losses and look to long-term gains.

Also not recommended by most investment advisors for retirement accounts are tax-exempt funds, which usually pay a slightly lower return, because their tax-free feature is wasted.

INVESTMENT PLANNING FOR RETIREMENT FUNDS 29

All retirement account withdrawals are taxed as ordinary income.

Diversifying your investments

You may set up a retirement plan and select one investment vehicle in that year and choose another the next year. You may also split your contribution between two or more investments. For example, you are eligible to contribute $2,000 to an IRA. You may choose to put $500 into a stock fund, $1,000 into an individual retirement account at your local bank, and $500 into a money market fund. But consider whether you will get the best return on your investment if you put less than $2,000 into a particular instrument. For example, some banks may limit the top interest rate to IRA accounts with the maximum contribution of $2,000. If you deposit only $1,000 in an IRA account, you may receive a lower interest rate.

IRA INVESTMENT OPTIONS

Institution	Investments	Return
Banks, thrifts, credit unions	Savings certificates	Tied to Treasury rates
	Passbook saving account	5¼% at commercial banks, 5½% at thrifts, higher at credit unions
Insurance companies	Fixed-premium front-load annuities	Fixed for one year at a time
	Back-load flexible premium annuities	Fluctuates
Brokerage	Self-directed: stocks, bonds, unit investment trusts, government obligations, limited partnerships	Fluctuates
	Load funds: funds investing in stocks, bonds, money market instruments, options, commodities	Fluctuates
Mutual fund families	No-load funds: funds investing in stocks, bonds, money market instruments, options, commodities	Fluctuates
	Load funds: funds investing in stocks, bonds, money market instruments, options, commodities	Fluctuates

Safety	Opening fees	Annual management fees	Withdrawal penalties
Guaranteed by FDIC/FSLIC	None	Generally none	Six months' interest on maturities of one year or more; no penalties at credit unions
Guaranteed by FDIC/FSLIC	None	None	None
	8%–9%	About $8–$10	None
	0–$30	About $25–$30	7%–8%; declines 1% each year and ends after first 7 to 10 years
No guarantee against market losses, your account is guaranteed by SIPC against mismanagement or insolvency of the firm	0–$30	$25–$50, plus commissions. Possibly a fee equal to a percentage of your portfolio	None
Guaranteed by SIPC	$15–$20	About $20, plus $5 to switch among funds	None
	0–$5	$10 or less; free switching	None
	6%–8½%	$10 or less; $5 to switch among funds	None

Chapter 2
YOUR IRA

THE tax shelter advantages of IRAs are designed to encourage every person who has earned income to save for retirement. You have earned income if you have wage or salary income or are self-employed as a business owner or professional.

Setting up an IRA is simple. You do not need special IRS approval for your plan as is generally necessary for Keogh and corporate retirement plans. Banks, brokerage firms, and insurance companies offering IRA investment plans will provide you with all necessary forms.

You may set up your IRA plan as an individual retirement account or an individual retirement annuity.

What is an individual retirement account?

Technically, an individual retirement account is a trust or custodial account. The trustee or custodian can be either the savings institution, brokerage firm, or mutual fund with which you have opened your IRA account. The trustee or custodian invests your funds according to the plan you have selected. Thus if you have invested in a certificate of deposit (CD) at your local bank, the bank acts as custodian for your CD. Generally, no fee is charged by a savings institution for an individual retirement account. The cost of other accounts is discussed in Chapter 1.

If you want a more active investment role, you may set up a "self-directed" plan. You make your own investment decisions while a bank, brokerage firm, or other institution or trustee handles your account. The fees for a self-directed plan may be high, so it may not pay to set up such an account until you have built up a sizable IRA fund.

You set up your self-directed plan following a Treasury model form. The model trust (Form 5305) and the model custodian account agreement (Form 5305A) meet the requirements of an exempt IRA. You do not need a ruling or determination letter approving the exemption of the account as is required of other qualified retirement plans. If you have a self-directed IRA, you may not invest in collectibles, such as coins, stamps, antique rugs, or artwork. Assets used to acquire collectibles are treated as distributions and are taxed to you.

What is an individual retirement annuity?

An individual retirement annuity is an annuity contract or an endowment contract issued by an insurance company which pays a specified amount monthly beginning at age 59½, or at retirement, and continuing for life. The annuity contract may be on your life or may be a joint and survivor contract for the benefit of you and your spouse. No trustee or custodian is required. The contract, endorsed to meet the terms of an IRA, is all that is required.

In the case of an endowment contract, no deduction is permitted for the portion of the premium allocable to life insurance. This nondeductible amount is referred to as P.S. 85 and will be supplied by your insurance agent.

The contract will not contain loan provisions because borrowing or pledging of the contract is not allowed under an IRA.

The contract must not have fixed premiums or annual premiums exceeding $2,000.

Insurance company fees for an IRA annuity may be steep, especially in the early years of the contract. Determine how much of your annual contribution is actually for the purchase of an annuity and how much covers insurance company charges.

IRA break-even point for younger workers

Younger workers, especially those facing large financial obligations, such as purchase of a home or business, or college education for their children, may be reluctant to tie up their funds in an IRA. There is good reason for hesitating. Current law imposes a 10% penalty for withdrawals before age 59½, except in

34 IRA, KEOGH, AND OTHER RETIREMENT PLANS

the case of disability. A tax law proposal would raise the penalty to 15%. However, the money is yours, and if you need it before age 59½ you may pay the penalty and still come out ahead, depending on your tax bracket, investment return, and how long you have been contributing.

If you are concerned about an early withdrawal, project the return on your IRA investment and figure, at a projected date of early withdrawal, the tax cost of a distribution increased by the penalty. Compare this net sum with the amount which you determine you would have earned on a similar investment not subject to the tax benefits of an IRA. The following examples are based on 1985 law.

EXAMPLE—

A person in his early twenties and in the 30% bracket invests $2,000 in a two-year IRA certificate earning 10% compounded daily. After two years, he needs the funds and withdraws the entire account balance of $2,443. His tax on the withdrawal is $977. This means he netted $1,466 on his $2,000 investment. This loss is attributed to the ordinary tax and penalty. If he had not invested in an IRA, he could have invested $1,400 in a regular account ($2,000 less $600 tax in the 30% bracket) at the same 10% rate. After two years, the regular account balance would be $1,617, $151 more than the IRA.

IRA account
Balance		$2,443
Less: Tax on $2,443 at 30%	$733	
Penalty	244	977
Return after taxes		$1,466

Savings account
Balance	$1,710
Less: Tax on interest	93
Return after taxes	$1,617

An IRA is the better choice only if withdrawals are delayed until the year in which the IRA gives a greater after-tax yield than the after-tax yield of a regular investment. Take the figure of the above example but stay in the 30% tax bracket—this point is not reached until the seventh year, assuming the same tax bracket and investment return. After seven years, the IRA account will show a balance of $4,027. If it is then withdrawn, tax will be $1,611, netting $2,416. A regular savings account would show a balance of $2,819, and the net on this account would be $2,393. Here the IRA in the seventh year starts to give a greater return.

IRA account
Balance		$4,027
Less: Tax on $4,027	$1,208	
Penalty	403	1,611
Return after taxes		$2,416

Regular account
Balance	$2,819
Less: Tax on interest	426
	$2,393

The spread in favor of the IRA widens the longer the IRA is kept intact.

Note that the 10% penalty applies only to distributions before age 59½ if a disability is not shown for making the distribution. If the 10% penalty does not apply, the IRA is a better investment after one year. For example, a person 60 years of age and in the 30% bracket, by investing in an IRA, would be ahead after one year.

IRA account
Balance at end of one year	$2,210
Less: Tax on withdrawal	663
Return after taxes	$1,547

Regular account
Balance at end of year	$1,547
Less: Tax on interest	44
Return after taxes	$1,503

Contributing to a company plan

Your company may provide an opportunity for you to make voluntary IRA contributions to the company plan. The advan-

36 IRA, KEOGH, AND OTHER RETIREMENT PLANS

tages of making voluntary contributions is that the funds are invested by the trustees of the plan. Distributions from employer-sponsored plans must begin by the April 1 following the year you reach age 70½ unless you continue working.

The rules for employer-sponsored IRA plans are generally the same as for personal IRAs. Distributions do not qualify for ten-year averaging. Penalties similar to those imposed under the IRA provisions are imposed on early withdrawal of deductible contributions from a qualified plan. Rollovers from an employer plan may be made to an IRA without incurring any withdrawal penalty, subject to the rule which limits rollovers to one per year.

Voluntary contributions to a company plan may not be made for your spouse. If you want to cover your spouse, you must set up an IRA outside of the company plan.

You do not have to count voluntary contributions to a company plan as your personal IRA deductible contribution. Voluntary contributions can accumulate tax free in the company fund while at the same time you can make a separate tax-deductible contribution to a personal IRA if you have additional available funds. If you follow this practice, you must specifically designate the voluntary contributions as nondeductible. Failure to make a designation automatically results in the treatment of voluntary contributions as deductible IRA contributions, thereby limiting the amount of IRA contributions you may make outside the plan. For example, your employer's plan allows you to make an annual voluntary contribution of $750. In 1986, you contribute $750 but do not designate the payment as nondeductible. You may then contribute only up to $1,250 ($2,000 − $750) to an IRA set up outside of the company plan for a total deduction of $2,000. If you designate the $750 as nondeductible, you may contribute and deduct up to $2,000 to your personal IRA.

Even though voluntary contributions are deductible, your employer is required to withhold FICA taxes on payroll deductions that go into the plan.

Check with your employer's plan administrator to determine when voluntary contributions must be made to avoid losing a contribution deduction. While you have until April 15, 1987, to make an IRA contribution for 1986, your employer is allowed, but not required, to treat contributions made in 1987 as 1986 contributions.

Figuring your contribution

Each year you may contribute and deduct 100% of your compensation up to $2,000 to an IRA. Thus if you work part time and earn $2,000, you may make the maximum IRA contribution. If both you and your spouse work, your total allowed deduction is $4,000. You may deduct the contribution whether or not you itemize deductions.

You do not have to contribute the maximum even though you are qualified to do so. You may contribute any amount you want up to the maximum. You may change your contribution each year, for example, contributing the maximum one year and a lesser amount the next. Be aware, however, that some high-yield investments are open only to those contributing $2,000. If you contribute less than the maximum one year, you may not make it up in a later year.

Different contribution limits apply to IRAs for nonworking spouses and IRAs for divorced persons, discussed later in this chapter.

Your deductible contribution must be based on payments received for rendering personal services, such as salary, wages, commissions, tips, fees, bonuses, or self-employed earned income. Net losses from self-employment do not reduce wages earned as an employee. Thus if you are employed and have a sideline business that suffers a loss, you may base an IRA contribution on your wages, regardless of the size of the loss. However, if your only income is from your unincorporated business which suffers a loss, you may not claim an IRA deduction.

Compensation does not include investment income, such as interest, dividends, or profits from sales of property. A trader whose sole income was derived from stock dividends and gains in buying and selling stocks set up an IRA and deducted his contribution. The IRS disallowed the deduction on the grounds that his income was not earned income. The trader argued that compensation is a broad term which should include his profits from investments. His trading activities were more extensive than those of a mere investor. Despite his substantial investment activities, the Tax Court sided with the IRS. His profits came from property holdings and are not considered earned income.

The IRS has stated in private letter rulings that compensation does not include disability payments, deferred compensation (e.g. incentive stock options, stock appreciation rights, and nonqualified stock options), or retirement pay.

You may not base an IRA contribution on income earned abroad for which the foreign earned income exclusion is claimed.

The compensation must actually be earned by you. If you live in a community-property state, the fact that one-half of your spouse's income is considered yours does not entitle you to make contributions to an IRA based on that income.

As long as you have earnings, you may contribute to an IRA even though you are receiving a pension or Social Security.

No deduction may be claimed for contributions to an inherited IRA, unless you inherited the IRA as the surviving spouse.

Age limit on contributions

There is no minimum age requirement for contributions to an IRA. Children with earnings are permitted to make contributions.

You may not deduct contributions made in the year you reach age 70½. Thus individuals born in June 1915 or earlier may not make IRA contributions for 1985. However, if your employer makes a contribution to your account under an SEP, you may claim a deduction (see Chapter 5).

Further, once you reach age 70½, you must begin to take distributions from your IRA by April 1 of the following year. If you make voluntary payments to your employer's qualified plan, you may not claim a deduction in the year you reach age 70½. Also, you must start taking distributions if you reach age 70½ unless you continue working.

When to make contributions

You may make your contribution until the due date for filing your returns. Thus a contribution for 1985 may be made any time during 1985 but no later than April 15, 1986. You may not make a contribution before the start of the calendar year; your 1986 contribution may not be made before January 1, 1986.

You do not have to make your entire contribution at once. You may contribute a small amount each month or several larger installments until you reach your maximum. Some banks will arrange with your employer to have your contributions made via payroll deductions. However, check whether your investment vehicle will accept periodic contributions. For example, if your IRA is in 18-month bank certificates and you contribute $1,000 in January when the rate is 11%, you will not automatically get the same rate on a $1,000 contribution in July. Your July contribution will earn interest at the then-prevailing rate.

Your available cash will influence the timing of your contributions. If you have the cash to make a contribution at any time, consider doing so as early in the year as possible because earnings will accumulate tax free. One bank has claimed that making contributions at the beginning rather than at the end of each year means that approximately $50,000 more will accumulate after 30 years of contributions.

IRAs for married couples

If both you and your spouse have earned income, each of you may set up an IRA account up to $2,000.

EXAMPLES—

1. You earn a salary of $20,000; your spouse earns $10,000. Both of you are eligible to set up IRAs. On a joint return the maximum deduction is $4,000. If only one of you works and qualifies to set up an IRA, the maximum deduction is $2,000, unless an account for a nonworking spouse is set up.
2. You live in a community-property state. You earn a salary of $20,000. Your spouse does not work. The maximum deduction for an IRA is $2,000, even though under the community-property laws your spouse is considered to have earned half your salary. You may set up an IRA for your nonworking spouse. In that case, your maximum deduction may not exceed $2,250.

Account for nonworking spouse. If you are eligible to contribute to an IRA, you may also make deductible contributions on behalf of your nonworking spouse. You may have two separate IRAs, one for you and one for your spouse, or a single IRA which has a subaccount for you and another subaccount for your spouse. A joint account is not allowed. However, each spouse may have a right of survivorship in the subaccount of the other.

Your maximum deduction for both accounts is $2,250; which may be divided between you however you wish so long as neither of you receives more than $2,000.

If you already have an IRA for yourself and you want to make contributions on behalf of your nonworking spouse, you may do so by opening a new IRA for your spouse and continuing your present IRA for yourself. However, if you have an annuity or endowment contract, check with your insurance agent about any contract restrictions on reducing your premium payments. Before setting up a single IRA with subaccounts for you and your spouse, check Treasury regulations covering their use.

If you set up an account (or a subaccount) for your spouse, your spouse must not have any compensation, including tax-exempt foreign earned income for the year. Suppose your spouse stopped working on December 31, 1985, and received a final paycheck on January 5, 1986. According to the IRS, under the spousal account rules you may not make a contribution in 1986 to your spouse's account even if your spouse is not employed at any time during 1986 because your spouse received pay during 1986. On the other hand your spouse may receive any amount of unearned income, such as interest, dividends, or Social Security benefits, and contributions on your spouse's behalf are deductible.

A working spouse over age 70½ may continue making contributions to the account of a nonworking spouse under age 70½. The contribution is limited to $2,000 and must be allocated to the account of the nonworking spouse.

If you are divorced, you may not maintain a spousal account for your former spouse. If you contributed to an account on behalf of your nonworking spouse and divorce later in the year, the contribution is an excess contribution. IRAs based on alimony are discussed below.

An amount distributed to one spouse may not be rolled over to an IRA account of the other spouse, except in the case of divorce.

IRAs for divorced persons

If you are divorced with little or no earnings but receive taxable alimony, you may make deductible IRA contributions equal to 100% of the taxable alimony but no more than $2,000. Taxable alimony is alimony paid under (1) a decree of divorce or separate maintenance or a written agreement incident to such a decree, (2) a written separation agreement, or (3) a decree of support.

A divorced spouse with earnings need not rely on the above rules but may make IRA contributions of 100% of earnings up to $2,000.

How distributions are taxed

All distributions from an IRA, whether paid in a lump sum or as an annuity, are taxed as ordinary income. Distributions do not qualify for special ten-year averaging. However, the regular five-year averaging method may be used to reduce the current tax.

Special retirement bonds. In the past, one IRA investment alternative was the purchase of special U.S. Retirement Bonds, which the Treasury stopped issuing on April 30, 1982. Proceeds are taxable in the year the bonds are redeemed. However, you must report the full proceeds in the year you reach age 70½ even if you do not redeem the bonds.

Activities that trigger distribution treatment. Certain investments or activities are forbidden to an IRA. If you engage in one, you are treated as if you received a distribution even though no funds were actually distributed to you.

An investment in collectibles by a self-directed IRA is treated as a distribution. Collectibles include art, rugs, antiques, gems, stamps, coins, and similar items.

If you use your IRA or part of it as security for a loan, the pledged portion is treated as a distribution. If you borrow from your IRA annuity, you are considered to have received the entire amount in your contract. Further, your IRA loses its tax-exempt status.

If you are charged with any of these distributions and you are not yet age 59½, you will be liable for a penalty for premature distributions, discussed later in this chapter.

Withholding. Tax is automatically withheld on IRA distributions, unless you make a special election to avoid withholding on the payments.

The party making the distribution must notify you of your right to avoid withholding. The Treasury has provided these notification guidelines: The payer must give notice of withholding options no later than the date of the first payment. The notice will instruct you that if the election is not made, income tax will be withheld as if you were married with three exemptions. No withholding is taken from nondeductible contributions you have made and on annual distributions of less than $5,400.

If you elect to avoid withholding, be sure that you do not run afoul of the estimated tax rules; otherwise you may be liable for a penalty.

Reporting requirements for IRAs

To date, you do not have to file any special forms with the IRS to report the opening of your IRA, contributions to your plans, or earnings on your contributions. You merely claim your contribution deduction on your tax return. Trustees report IRA contributions to the IRS on Form 5498.

By June 30 of each year, your IRA custodian or trustee is required to furnish you with a statement of contributions, rollovers, and year-end account values. Some banks or other custodians or trustees give reports more frequently.

Reporting is required if you make a tax-free rollover. The rollover is reported on your tax return for information purposes. To date, no special form has been required; a line on Form 1040 may be used.

Reporting is also required if you are liable for a penalty for premature withdrawals, excess contributions, or insufficient withdrawals. You file Form 5329 with your return if you are liable for any of these penalties. Failure to file Form 5329 may result in an additional penalty of $10 per day (up to a maximum of $5,000).

Bank penalties on closing time-deposit accounts before maturity

If you invest your IRA funds in a time-deposit account or savings certificate at a bank, you may have to pay a penalty if you close the account before maturity. If the term of the account is one year or less, the penalty is one month's interest. If it is more than one year, the penalty is three months' interest.

The penalty may be waived in certain circumstances. Banks are also permitted to waive the penalty for those age 59½ and over; most banks have chosen to do so. There is no penalty at credit unions.

Depending on how long the account has been open, a penalty may result in the forfeiture of some principal.

EXAMPLE—

You invest your $2,000 IRA contribution in a 2½-year savings certificate earning 12% compounded monthly. You wish to withdraw your money after two months. Your account has earned $40 interest. Your penalty is three months' interest, or $60. The balance of the penalty, $20 ($60 − $40), will be deducted from principal.

When interest rates rise and your money is tied up in a low-interest account, ask the bank to determine whether it pays you to incur the penalty by closing out the account and transferring your funds to an account paying higher interest.

EXAMPLE—

You invested $2,000 in a 10% four-year account of which there remains a term of 2½ years. You have the option of switching to a 14% 2½-year account. Interest in both accounts is compounded annually. If you held the 10% account to maturity, you would have $2,928. However, if you switch to the 14% account, you would have $3,166 even after paying a penalty of $50.

Avoiding excess contribution penalties

Contributions over allowable amounts are penalized. If you contribute more than the amount allowed as a deduction, the excess contribution may be subject to a penalty tax of 6%. The penalty tax is cumulative. That is, unless you correct the excess, you will be subject to another penalty in the following year on the excess contribution. The penalty tax is not deductible.

EXAMPLE—

You contribute $2,000 to an IRA earning 10%, but you were only entitled to contribute $1,500 because you earned only $1,500 from part-time work. Your penalty is $30 (6% of the $500 excess contribution) unless you correct the contribution.

The penalty tax on excess contributions may be avoided as follows: (1) An excess contribution, if not larger than $2,250 and if a deduction for the excess was not allowed, may be withdrawn at any time and the distribution treated as if it were never contributed (contributions in excess of $2,250 must be withdrawn prior to the due date for filing your return in order to avoid a penalty). (2) If an excess rollover contribution was made because of reliance on erroneous information, the $2,250 limitation is increased to the extent of the excess contribution attributable to the erroneous information. (3) Excess contributions which are not withdrawn may be deducted in later years in which there is an unused deduction limitation. Higher excess contribution limits apply for SEP contributions.

EXAMPLE—

In 1985 you contributed $1,500, but you were entitled to contribute only $1,200. If you are entitled to deduct $2,000 in 1986, you may correct your excess 1985 contribution by undercontributing $300. Your deduction for 1985 is $1,200. Your deduction for 1986 is $2,000 (the $1,700 you actually contributed in 1985 plus the carryover of the excess contribution from 1984).

Premature distributions may be subject to penalty

The law imposes a penalty if you withdraw IRA funds before age 59½ and are not disabled. You will be subject to a penalty tax of 10% on the premature distribution even if the money is needed for an emergency. The 10% tax is in addition to the tax that will be incurred when you include the distribution as ordinary income with your other income.

EXAMPLE—

An unmarried man, age 40, withdraws $3,000 from his IRA plan. Assume that after including the $3,000 distribution in income, he is in the 35% tax bracket. Tax on the distribution is $1,050 (35% of $3,000). To this amount he must add 10% of $3,000, or $300. His total tax on the distribution is $1,350, leaving him a net distribution of $1,650 ($3,000 − $1,350).

The penalty may be increased to 15%.

Redemption of U.S. Retirement Bonds before age 59½ is considered a premature distribution.

The penalty is figured only with reference to age and has nothing to do with actual retirement. Thus if you retire at age 58 and take a distribution, you are subject to a penalty.

If you borrow on your annuity contract, you are considered to have received your entire interest. Borrowing will subject the fair market value of the contract to tax at ordinary income rates as of the first day of the taxable year of the borrowing. Your IRA loses its tax-exempt status. As a practical matter, you are prohibited from borrowing since your contract may not contain a loan provision.

If you use the account or part of it as security for a loan, the pledged portion is treated as a distribution. The payment of an overdue premium in the form of a loan against the cash surrender value of the contract is considered a distribution. A taxable rollover contribution, such as a second rollover within a 12-month period, is subject to a penalty if you are not age 59½. See Chapter 8 for further details.

You will not be liable for a premature distribution if you are correcting an excess contribution that did not exceed $2,250.

How much must you withdraw after age 70½?

The law requires that you start receiving distributions from your account after age 70½. By the April 1 after the date you reach age 70½, you must start to receive minimum distributions to avoid a penalty tax. The penalty applies to the difference between the amount you should have received and the amount you did receive.

The required installment amount is generally fixed by the amount of the account and your life expectancy. The IRS provides life expectancy figures. If you are married, you may figure the minimum distribution on the basis of the joint life expectancies of you and your spouse. Minimum distributions may also be based on the joint life expectancy of you and a beneficiary other than a spouse.

The minimum distribution may be refigured each year to keep step with your life expectancy until the fund is exhausted. *Refiguring your life expectancy annually is an advantage if you want to take smaller distributions and conserve the principal.* If you base distributions on the joint life expectancy of you and your spouse, you may also recalculate your joint life expectancy annually. If payouts are figured over the joint lives of yourself and someone other than your spouse, you may refigure only your life expectancy each year; the life expectancy of the beneficiary is determined as of the year you begin distributions. Further, where payouts are figured over the joint lives of you and a younger beneficiary, there is a limit as to how much you can minimize distributions. Under an "incidental benefits" test, you must withdraw at least 50% of the minimum amount required based on your life expectancy alone. However, this 50% test does not apply to distributions under a qualified joint and survivor annuity with your spouse.

Life expectancy figures are taken from IRS annuity tables. The trustee of your IRA can also give you the figures and help you compute the minimum required installment.

If you are age 70½, working, and have an SEP-IRA, you must still begin to receive distributions even though your employer is making contributions to your account.

If you have a spousal IRA and you are age 70½ but your

spouse is younger, your spouse does not have to receive distributions.

Payments to beneficiaries. If an IRA owner dies before receiving his or her entire IRA interest, the balance must be distributed to the beneficiaries at least as rapidly as under the method the owner was using. If the owner dies before receiving any benefits and the surviving spouse is beneficiary, he or she may delay withdrawals until the date the owner would have reached age 70½; then, the account must be distributed over the surviving spouse's life or life expectancy. If someone other than a surviving spouse is beneficiary, the account balance must generally be distributed within five years but an exception allows payments to be spread over the beneficiary's life or a period not extending beyond the beneficiary's life expectancy. For this exception to apply, distributions must begin no later than one year after the date of the owner's death.

The IRS may waive the penalty for insufficient withdrawals if due to reasonable error and if steps are being taken to remedy the situation. You must submit evidence to account for shortfalls in withdrawals and show you are rectifying the situation. The IRS has indicated that examples of acceptable reasons for insufficient withdrawals include erroneous advice from the sponsoring organization or other pension advisors or that your own good-faith efforts to apply the required withdrawal formula produced a miscalculation. Attach your letter of explanation to Form 5329. You must pay the penalty tax; if the IRS grants you a waiver, it will refund the penalty.

Recordkeeping for your IRA

Over the course of your working career you may contribute tens of thousands of dollars to your IRA. However, in all likelihood all your money will not be in one place. Further, you may move a considerable distance from your present home and could lose sight of a CD or other IRA investment. It is imperative that you establish a recordkeeping system to keep track of your IRA investments, to check their yields, and in the case of your death, to assist your heirs in collecting benefits. Thus you should note these points:

48 IRA, KEOGH, AND OTHER RETIREMENT PLANS

1. When will you have to reinvest your fund? That is, when will your CD mature or your investment trust mature?

2. What are the penalties for terminating an investment before the end of a set term (bank penalties for premature withdrawals; insurance company penalties for canceling an annuity)?

3. Who have you named as beneficiary and what payout methods have you selected?

Here is a form for keeping your IRA information in order. A separate form should be used for each investment.

Type of IRA _____ Account #_____

Trustee or custodian: _____

Address of trustee or custodian: _____

Beneficiary _____

Other information (Maturity date, interest rate, etc.) _____

Date	Contribution	Earnings on contribution	Withdrawals	Balance

Chapter 3
YOUR SELF-EMPLOYMENT RETIREMENT PLAN

IF you are in business yourself or in partnership with others and you want to provide for your retirement, the advantages of setting up a self-employed retirement or Keogh plan flow from:

1. Tax deductions claimed for contributions made to the plan;
2. Accumulations of tax-free income earned on assets held by the plan; and
3. Special averaging provisions for benefits paid on retirement.

To help you decide whether you should set up a Keogh plan, compare an estimate of the amount that a regular investment program would return to you on retirement with an estimate of the amount the Keogh plan would provide. If your comparison is based on a savings plan at a fixed rate of return, there is no question that the Keogh plan will give a greater return because of the tax benefits provided by the law. However, you should also consider these points before making your decision:

1. *Inclusion of employees in the plan.* Generally, you must include your full-time employees in your Keogh plan and contribute funds for their retirement account. However, your contributions to their accounts are deductible, thus reducing the cost of your contribution.

If you have a large payroll, the cost of including your employees may eliminate the tax savings on your account. This possibility must be calculated in each case. The cost of including employees in a retirement plan may be balanced by increased goodwill.

2. *The amount of cash available for contributions.* After

meeting both your personal and business expenses, do you have cash to put into the fund? You may solve part of this problem by providing that the plan has a variable formula of contributions to meet fluctuations in income.

If you set up a Keogh plan prior to 1984, you may wish to amend your plan to take advantage of the more favorable current contribution limits, discussed below.

3. *The availability of funds for emergencies.* You will be subject to a penalty on distributions before you reach age 59½ unless you are disabled or you are a partner with an interest of 5% or less.

Are you eligible to start a Keogh plan?

You may set up a Keogh plan if you earn self-employment income through your performance of personal services. For purposes of a Keogh plan, earned income is your net profit (gross business or professional income less allowable business deductions). Earned income may be from your main occupation or from a sideline business. Income earned abroad and excluded from federal income tax is not considered earned income for purposes of the plan. If you are an inactive owner, such as a limited partner or a retired partner receiving distributions from the partnership, you may not make contributions to a Keogh plan.

An individual partner, although self-employed, may not set up a personal Keogh plan. The plan must be established by the partnership.

If you control more than one business (own more than 50% of the capital or profits interest in a partnership or the entire share of an unincorporated business), the following rules apply: (1) You must set up plans for all businesses under your control. These may be incorporated in one plan or remain separate. (2) Any additional plans must also conform to all regulations governing the original plan. (3) The additional plans must make contributions in an equal ratio and provide equal benefits.

These rules prevent you from increasing the maximum deductible contribution for your own benefit by contributing to more than one retirement plan. However, if you are an employee-member of a company retirement plan, you may set up a Keogh plan if you carry on a self-employed enterprise or profession on the side. For example, you are an attorney employed by a company that has a qualified pension plan of which you are a member. At the same time you have a practice on the side. You may set up a Keogh plan based on your self-employment earnings. Each plan is independent of the other.

A plan may not discriminate in terms of participation or benefits in favor of highly compensated personnel. Benefits must be for the employees and their beneficiaries, and their plan rights may not be subject to forfeiture. A plan may not allow any of its funds to be diverted for purposes other than pension benefits. Contributions made on your behalf may not exceed the ratio of contributions made on behalf of employees.

Choosing a plan

There are two general types of Keogh plans: defined-benefit plans and defined-contribution plans. A defined-benefit plan provides in advance for a specific retirement benefit funded by contributions based on an IRS formula and actuarial assumption.

The maximum annual retirement benefit is $90,000. This ceiling may be reduced by new law proposals.

A defined-benefit plan may prove costly if you have older employees who also must be provided with proportionate defined benefits. Further, the plan requires you to contribute to their accounts even if you do not have profits.

Under a defined-contribution plan, retirement benefits will depend on the contributions made to your account and the accounts of your employees over the years the plan is in force. If contributions are geared to profits, the plan is a profit-sharing plan. If contributions are not based on the profits, the plan is a money-purchase pension plan; for example, a plan which provides that contributions to employees' accounts are to be based on a percentage of their pay is a money-purchase pension plan. If you set up such a plan, you must contribute to their accounts even though you do not have earnings and are not permitted to contribute to your account. On the other hand if the contribution formula to both your account and the account of your employees is based on earning profits, you make contributions to your account and your employees' accounts only in profitable years. In a loss year you are not required to make contributions.

Choosing the funding structure for your Keogh plan

You must formally set up your plan in writing on or before the end of the taxable year in which you want the plan to be effective.

If you are interested in following an aggressive investment policy for funds in your Keogh plan, you will set up a trust to receive Keogh contributions. You may appoint a bank or trust company as the trustee. You may name yourself or an independent trustee to oversee the plan. Prior to 1984, owner-employees were prohibited from serving as trustees of their own plans.

As an owner-employee, your dealings with the trust are subject to restrictions. You are subject to penalties if you borrow from the trust, buy or lease property from or sell or lease property to the trust, or charge any fees for services rendered to the trust. These restrictions apply also to any member of your immediate family and any corporation in which you own more than half the voting stock, directly or indirectly.

If you are considering an investment in savings certificates, you need not set up a trust; you may use a custodial account with the bank.

If you use funds to buy nontransferable annuity contracts from an insurance company, no trust is necessary. Premium payments are made directly to the insurance company. The annuity contract may pay a fixed monthly income for life or a fixed period of years, or may be a variable annuity contract.

Defined-contribution limitations

In general, the contribution limits for self-employed individuals are similar to corporate plan limitations: the lower of 25% of earned income or $30,000. However, for purposes of figuring contributions, earned income is net earnings from self-employment less the deductible Keogh contribution. Because net earnings must be reduced by the deductible contribution, the maximum contribution for a money purchase plan is reduced from 25% to 20% of net earnings (before Keogh deduction is considered). You may deduct the entire 20% contribution. However, if you have a profit-sharing plan, you may not claim a 20% deduction. The maximum deductible profit-sharing contribution is technically 15% of earned income but because net earnings must be reduced, your maximum deductible contribution is reduced from 15% to 13.0435% of your net earnings (before Keogh deduction is considered). To maximize your deductible contributions, you may establish a separate money purchase plan to supplement a profit-sharing plan. A bank or other Keogh plan trustee can help you set up separate plans.

The $30,000 ceiling may be reduced to $25,000 by a new law proposal.

Defined-benefit contribution limitations

A defined-benefit plan allows you to build up retirement benefits equal to a percentage of your earnings.

In 1984 and later years, the limitations on contributions to defined-benefit Keogh plans follow the rules applied to similar corporate plans. The maximum annual retirement benefit may not exceed $90,000. The contribution limitation is the amount actuarially determined to provide that benefit upon retirement. The $90,000 ceiling would be reduced by a tax law proposal.

You may not take advantage of a defined-benefit plan unless it provides benefits for all your employees without taking into account benefits under Social Security. All plans of a controlled group of businesses are aggregated for purposes of the limitations applied to defined benefits.

To assure reasonable comparability between defined benefit and defined contribution and combinations of plans, the regulations provide for appropriate adjustments in the allowable amount of deductible contribution, or permissible rate of benefit accruals in cases where the same self-employed individual is a participant in two or more plans.

Other rules for defined-benefit plans are explained in Chapter 4.

When to make annual contributions

Contributions may be made until the due date for your tax return (plus extensions). Thus contributions for 1986 may be made at any time during 1986 and until April 15, 1987. However, a written plan must be set up no later than the end of the year. If you are on a calendar year and have not established your Keogh plan by December 31, you may not contribute to it for that year.

While it is advantageous to make contributions as early as possible to permit earnings to accumulate tax free, as a practical matter you may be forced to delay making contributions until the end of the year. This will allow you to figure your earnings, the compensation of your employees upon which contributions will be based, and in the case of a profit-sharing plan, your profits.

Including employees in your plan

You may not set up a qualified plan solely for your personal benefit. Your employees must be entitled to enter the plan. You may require that a new employee work for a length of time and reach a certain age before being eligible to participate. However, you may not exclude an employee who has reached age 21 with at least one year of service. If your plan provides for full and immediate vesting of benefits, an employee may be required to complete three years of service before participating. You are not required to cover seasonal or part-time employees who work less than 1,000 hours during a 12-month period. If you set up a defined-benefit plan, you may exclude an employee who is within five years of normal retirement age (which may not be later than age 65) when his or her period of service begins.

You may select a permissible vesting schedule under which an employee's right to benefits becomes nonforfeitable. Vesting schedules are discussed in Chapter 8. However, if your plan is considered top heavy because it disproportionately favors you, other owners, and key personnel (as explained in Chapter 4), you must adopt a stricter vesting schedule.

YOUR SELF-EMPLOYMENT RETIREMENT PLAN

You must furnish to your employees written notice of the plan, including a description of its features.

Your contributions on behalf of your employees are deductible.

Voluntary contributions may allow for increased tax-free accumulations

You may set up a plan which permits you and your employees to make additional *voluntary* contributions up to 10% of income to your account and to theirs. Although you and your employees may not deduct voluntary contributions, there is an advantage: earnings on the fund accumulate tax free.

When can you receive retirement benefits?

Distributions before age 59½ are subject to a 10% penalty in years starting after 1984 if you own more than a 5% interest and are not totally disabled.

The penalty may be raised to 15% by a new tax law proposal.

You may redeem a U.S. Retirement bond (purchased before May 1, 1982) before age 59½ and avoid tax by making a rollover within 60 days to an IRA.

You are considered disabled if you cannot engage in substantial gainful activity because of an illness that can be expected to be of long and indefinite duration or to result in death.

If you hold more than a 5% interest in your business, you must start to receive distributions by April 1 following the calendar year in which you reach age 70½, even if you do not retire. If you have an interest of 5% or less, you may delay distributions until April 1 following the calendar year of retirement.

Distributions may be spread over your life or life expectancy, or over the joint lives or life expectancies of you and any designated beneficiary. You may annually recalculate your life expectancy, or the joint life expectancy of you and your spouse. This allows you to spread payments over a longer period because life expectancy increases as you get older. Although you may reduce the required minimum distribution by spreading payments over the joint life expectancies of you and a younger beneficiary other than your spouse, you cannot reduce distributions below a certain amount. Under an "incidental benefits" test, your withdrawal method must provide for distributions over your life expectancy that exceed 50% of your account. This 50% test does not apply to distributions taken as a qualified joint and survivor annuity with your spouse.

Your employees are also subject to a distribution age test. They must start to receive distributions by the April 1 following the *later* of the year they reach age 70½ or retire. Thus, unlike a more than 5% owner, rank and file employees who work past age 70½ may delay the start of distributions until they retire.

Note: A tax proposal would phase out the rule allowing delay until the year of retirement.

Voluntary contributions (nondeductible contributions, if permitted) made after September 2, 1974, may be withdrawn at any time without regard to age.

If you are married, benefits must generally be in the form of a qualified joint and survivor annuity; see Chapter 4.

Payments to beneficiaries. If you die after you begin to receive benefits, the balance of your benefits must be distributed to your beneficiary at least as rapidly as under the method you used. The beneficiary may accelerate payments. If death occurs before you received any benefits, the entire interest must be distributed to beneficiaries within five years but there are exceptions. If a surviving spouse is the beneficiary, payments do not have to begin until the date on which the plan participant would have reached age 70½; then, payments may be distributed over the surviving spouse's life or life expectancy. Payments to a surviving spouse under a qualified joint and survivor annuity are also exempt from the general five-year rule.

If the beneficiary is a person other than a surviving spouse, payments may be spread over the beneficiary's life or life expectancy, provided the payments begin within one year of death; the one-year deadline may be extended by the IRS if circumstances warrant.

Pre-1984 distribution rules continue to apply if you made a special election before 1984.

Beneficiaries of self-employed individuals who die in 1984 or later years are entitled to claim the $5,000 death benefit exclusion for a lump-sum distribution from the plan.

YOUR SELF-EMPLOYMENT RETIREMENT PLAN 57

Incidental life insurance coverage

Some life insurance coverage may be purchased through a Keogh plan, provided it is considered incidental to the plan. However, you may not deduct contributions that are allocable to the insurance. Further, your basis in the policy is considered zero and thus your beneficiary may not use the cost to offset income attributable to the policy's cash value before death. Life insurance is considered incidental if it is not more than 100 times the monthly annuity, such as $1,000 of life insurance for each $10 of monthly annuity. If a defined-contribution plan includes term life insurance, the premium may not be more than 25% of a contribution. If whole-life insurance is used and half of the premium is for insurance protection and half for a cash reserve, the limit is 50% of contributions.

Despite contribution limitation increases after 1983, these limits on insurance coverage continue to apply.

How benefits are taxed

The way benefits are paid, whether in a lump sum or as an annuity, determines how benefits will be taxed. The method of payment is usually provided in the plan. For example, if your Keogh plan invested in an annuity, you would receive annuity payments.

Lump-sum distributions. If you receive a lump-sum distribution, you may treat the portion attributable to pre-1974 years as long-term capital gain; the portion of a distribution allocable to 1974 and later years is taxable as ordinary income. To qualify for capital gain treatment you must elect to use the ten-year averaging computation for the ordinary income portion. To elect the ten-year averaging method you must have participated in the plan for at least five years. If your capital gains are taxed at a higher tax rate than that of the ten-year averaging method, you may forgo capital gain treatment and treat your entire distribution as ordinary income subject to the ten-year averaging method.

A lump-sum distribution may be rolled over to an IRA to avoid current taxation.

Rollover of partial distributions. If you receive a distribution after July 18, 1984 that equals at least 50% of your plan account balance, you may elect to roll it over to an IRA, provided it is not one of a series of periodic payments. The rollover must be made within 60 days. Under the 50% test, you may disregard amounts credited to you under other qualified plans maintained by the same employer. If you elect to roll over, a later distribution of your entire account balance will not qualify for 10-year averaging or capital gain treatment. A surviving spouse who receives a qualifying partial distribution may also make a rollover to an IRA.

Note: A tax law proposal would repeal ten-year averaging and replace it with a five-year averaging method.

U.S. retirement bonds

A redemption of a U.S. retirement bond bought before May 1, 1982 (when the Treasury ceased issuing them) does not qualify for 10-year averaging or capital gain treatment, even if redemption is in a lump sum. The redemption proceeds are ordinary income.

You may redeem the bonds before age 59½ although the terms of the bond when issued prohibited redemption before age 59½ except for disability or death. Tax may be avoided on the redemption proceeds by making a timely rollover to an IRA or to another qualified pension or profit-sharing plan. If a rollover of redemption proceeds is made to a qualified plan and is later distributed as part of a lump-sum distribution, the rolled-over amount does not qualify for 10-year averaging or capital gain for the pre-1974 portions.

Annuity payments. These are taxable except for payments allocable to your investment in the policy. Your deductible contributions are not considered an investment in the policy. You have an investment if you made voluntary contributions.

Withholding on distributions. Payers of pensions are required to withhold on distributions unless you elect otherwise. Withholding rules are discussed in Chapter 7.

Penalties

A Keogh plan entails certain reporting requirements. The failure to observe them may result in substantial penalties. Similarly, penalties may be imposed for borrowing from the plan, premature distributions, and for excess contributions.

Penalty for failure to file annual report. The penalty for failing to file the annual comprehensive report is $25 a day until it is filed (maximum penalty $15,000). The penalty will be waived upon a showing that the delay was due to reasonable cause. You must file an annual information return even if you are the only plan participant. For plan years beginning before 1984, sole participants did not have to file an information return.

Form 5500-C must be filed for the first reporting year and once every third year. If a Form 5500-C has been filed for one of the two prior years, you may file a shorter form—Form 5500-R. Form 5500-C must be filed for the final plan year.

The information return must be filed with the IRS by the last day of the seventh month following the end of the plan year. Thus, if you have a calendar year plan, you must file your 1986 plan year return by July 31, 1987. You may apply for a filing extension of up to 2½ months on Form 5558; good cause must be shown. If your tax year and the plan tax year coincide, and you obtain a filing extension for your personal income tax return to a date later than the due date for the Form 5500-C (or 5500-R), that extension also applies to the Form 5500-C or R.

The IRS may simplify the above reporting rules for 1986.

Penalty for borrowing from the plan. Owners-employees who take loans from their Keogh account are subject to a 5% penalty and a 100% penalty. On Form 5330, you are required to report the loans and pay the 5% penalty based on an interest factor. The 100% penalty may be avoided by repaying the loan within 90 days of receiving an IRS deficiency notice.

Penalty for distributions before age 59½. Starting in 1985, the 10% premature withdrawal penalty applies to a distribution received before age 59½ to the extent attributable to years in which you owned more than 5% of your business. The penalty applies only to the taxable portion of a distribution. Your contributions may be withdrawn at any time without penalty.

The penalty does not apply if you are totally disabled. A person is considered totally disabled if he or she is unable to engage in any substantial gainful activity because of a physical or mental condition which has lasted or is expected to last for a long period or is expected to lead to death. You are not disabled if with reasonable effort and safety the condition can be alleviated so that you can hold a job.

If you receive a premature distribution before age 59½, the 10% penalty is imposed on that part of the distribution that exceeds your contributions, if any. The penalty is in addition to the regular income tax figured on the distribution. The penalty is not treated as part of the regular tax. Thus, it may not be reduced by any tax credits and may not be considered in figuring the alternative minimum tax.

Before 1984, a premature distribution also disqualified you for five years from having contributions made to your account. This rule does not apply after 1983.

Loans after August 13, 1982 are taxed as distributions only if they exceed the limits for loans from corporate plans, discussed in Chapter 4.

The IRS has ruled that a tax-free rollover may be made if the Keogh plan is terminated. A timely rollover will avoid the 10% penalty on premature distributions from top-heavy plans if the recipient is under 59½.

A new law proposal would impose a 15% penalty on premature distributions starting in 1986.

Excess contributions. Beginning in 1984, there is no excess contribution penalty tax. However, if contributions exceed the limits for defined-contribution plans or defined-benefit plans discussed in this chapter, your plan could be disqualified and no deductions would be allowed.

Proposed excess distribution penalty. A tax law proposal would impose a 15% penalty tax on annual distributions from all qualified plans (including IRAs) in excess of $112,500.

How to qualify your plan

You may set up your plan and contribute to it without advance IRS approval. As a practical matter, advance approval is advisable to avoid disqualification at some later date. Thus you may ask the district director for the district in which your business is located to review your plan. If you are setting up a trust you will need to consult an attorney versed in the field to prepare the trust agreement and to submit a request for IRS approval.

If you join a master or prototype plan, plan approval is simple. The sponsoring organization submits to the IRS Form 3672 for a defined-contribution plan or Form 3672A for a defined-benefit plan. When the master or prototype is approved, a number is assigned to the plan. The sponsoring organization then advises participating employers of the full name of the plan, the date of the favorable opinion letter, and the plan number.

Amendments to plans to conform them to changes in the law do not generally require determination letters or opinion letters.

Be sure to have existing plans reviewed and updated to reflect changes made by the 1982 Tax Act, particularly the top-heavy plan rules (*see* Chapter 4).

Deducting costs of a plan

Fees charged for setting up a Keogh plan are deductible as ordinary business expenses. If possible, pay trustee and actuary fees directly from your business rather than through plan contributions.

Eliminating restrictions on plans for owner-employees

A person who owns more than 10% of the capital interests or 10% of the profits of a business is an owner-employee. Prior to 1984, special rules applied to plans covering owner-employees. Only large partnerships in which no one partner

62 IRA, KEOGH, AND OTHER RETIREMENT PLANS

owned more than a 10% interest were free from these restrictive rules. Beginning in 1984, there are no longer special restrictions for plans with owner-employees. Plans may be amended to delete any of the following restrictions but are not required to do so.

A plan with an owner-employee was required to use as its trustee an institution or other qualified person. Now the trustee is not required to be a bank or other institution and may be the owner-employee.

Immediate vesting of benefits or contributions made on behalf of employees other than owner-employees is no longer required. The plan may adopt any vesting schedule within the parameters of vesting requirements for qualified plans, as explained in Chapter 8.

A pension plan covering owner-employees could not be integrated with Social Security benefits except under special rules. Now, integration may be used. This greatly reduces the cost of contributions.

Chapter 4
YOUR CORPORATE RETIREMENT PLAN

Setting up a qualified company retirement plan

IF you have incorporated your business, setting up a qualified company retirement plan makes sound tax and investment sense. Your company receives a current deduction for contributions made to the plan, and you and other covered employees are not taxed on company contributions. Income earned on the contributions accumulates tax free. Tax is incurred when benefits are received. The results of tax-free compounding are illustrated in Chapter 1.

If you have employees, you must balance your personal benefits against the cost of including employees in the plan. A plan cannot qualify unless it provides for full-time employees. Further, top-heavy plans which favor stockholders or highly paid executives must pay minimum benefits to other employees. Against the cost of covering employees, consider the goodwill created by providing employee benefits. In addition to contribution costs you must also consider the costs of plan administration, which may be substantial, in your decision to set up a retirement plan.

When setting up a company plan, these important decisions must be made:

1. What type of retirement plan should I select: a pension plan or a deferred profit-sharing plan?
2. How much will the company contribute to the plan?
3. Should the plan allow for voluntary contributions?

4. When will employees be permitted to enter the plan?
5. When will employee benefits vest?
6. What happens to benefits when an employee terminates employment?
7. When must employees retire?

This chapter explains the kinds of company retirement plans, options you may select, and procedures you must follow. As a general observation, the laws governing pension plans are extremely technical, and you should consult an expert in the field before establishing a retirement program.

Recent law changes have generally reduced the benefits available under corporate plans, and since 1984 there is, in general, parity between the benefits available under corporate retirement and self-employed plans. Thus, there is no longer an incentive for professionals to incorporate in order to obtain retirement benefit advantages. Review your plan with your pension consultant to determine the implications and impact of these law changes.

Should you start a pension or profit-sharing plan?

Only a qualified retirement plan enjoys tax deductions for contributions, tax-free accumulations of income, and special tax treatment for distributions. A qualified plan is one that the IRS approves as having met certain standards concerning eligibility, benefits, and reporting.

A corporation may choose from several types of qualified retirement plans: pension plan, profit-sharing plan, stock-bonus plan, thrift plan, or a combination of plans. In general, only pension and profit-sharing plans are discussed in this book.

A pension plan is designed to provide a fixed benefit upon retirement. There are two types of pension plans. In a defined-benefit plan, the level of benefits is fixed and contributions are geared to provide those benefits at retirement. In a defined-contribution plan, it is the contributions that are fixed, and benefits depend on the size of the contributions and the number of years before retirement. Both types of pension plans differ from profit-sharing plans in that contributions must be made, regardless of profits.

If your corporation chooses a defined-benefit plan, the first step is deciding on a formula for determining benefits. Benefits are often based on years of service and a percentage of earnings over a certain period. For example, a plan may provide for a pension equal to a small percentage (1% or 2%) of an employee's average compensation during the last five years before retirement multiplied by years of service. For high earners, the pension allowed by the plan may have to be reduced because the law limits the annual benefit payable by defined-benefit plans, discussed below.

Once the benefit formula is determined, the company will actuarially compute the level of contributions needed to provide the funds to pay the anticipated benefits. Contributions must be made, regardless of profits. To determine annual contributions, an actuary will consider your age, earnings, and years before reaching retirement. Earnings of the fund may also affect contributions. If the fund earns more than the rate assumed when the plan was set up, the company may decrease its contributions; the IRS could require increased contributions if the plan did not earn as much as had been assumed.

In a defined-contribution plan, such as a money-purchase pension plan, the company commits itself to make a fixed annual contribution, regardless of profits. For example, a money-purchase plan may require contributions equal to 10% of each participant's annual salary. Contributions plus earnings on the fund will determine benefits.

In general, the money-purchase plan is favored if the employees are relatively young, since retirement benefits depend on the number of years they are in the plan. Older employees with fewer years until retirement prefer a defined-benefit plan which can set benefits at the maximum allowed by law.

Unlike a pension plan, a profit-sharing plan does not have fixed benefits. Contributions are made out of corporate profits and allocated to the employees participating in the plan according to a definite formula. The allocation must not discriminate in favor of stockholders, officers, and executives. At retirement or other payout date (upon disability, for example), the employee receives the amount allocated to his or her account plus the income and capital appreciation attributable to the allocated amount. A profit-sharing plan is a type of defined-contribution plan. The retirement benefits will be whatever the accumulated amount of contributions can buy upon retirement.

A pension plan should be considered only if the earnings record of your business shows a reasonable amount of stability. Pension plans call for regular contributions by your company, regardless of profits. A pension plan must be actuarially sound; the contributions must be sufficient to pay a fixed monthly sum to an employee who reaches retirement age and retires. To meet this obligation, the law imposes minimum standards; contributions are figured accordingly.

A profit-sharing plan is more flexible since your company is not obligated to pay a fixed annual amount into the fund. It may contribute according to a formula keyed to profits. In loss years, it may contribute nothing, while in prosperous years contributions can be substantial. Profit-sharing plans furnish employee incentives to increase profits, whereas pension plans furnish the employee security through fixed and prearranged future benefits.

The selection of a particular plan depends on your projection of future business conditions. Other factors to be weighed are the rate of labor turnover, the ratio of young to older employees, and the tax burden. Pension plans favor older employees; profit-sharing plans favor younger employees.

Pension plans are more costly to administer. In addition to fees for actuarial computations, you are required to pay premiums to the Pension Benefit Guaranty Corporation on behalf of each employee covered by a pension plan. Premiums cover retirement benefits for plans that fail or end before benefits are fully funded.

Pension plans and profit-sharing plans must provide for a trustee, except in the case of an annuity pension plan in which contracts are bought from an insurance company. If you set up a pension plan and fund it by buying an annuity contract, you give up all control over the investment of plan funds. The insurance company handles the investments and guarantees payment of stipulated benefits.

If you use a trustee plan, your plan involves the creation of a trust which is responsible for the investment and payment of funds contributed to it. You may name yourself trustee and you will be subject to fiduciary responsibility rules.

Overall limits on retirement contributions and benefits

Contribution limits are fixed according to the type of retirement plan involved.

Defined-benefit plans. The dollar limitation on annual benefits is $90,000. The $90,000 limit applies if it is less than the percentage limitation, which is 100% of average compensation for the employee's highest three consecutive earning years. If benefits are not paid in the form of a straight-life annuity, such as when a lump-sum distribution is made, the benefit must be made actuarially equivalent to the defined-benefit limitations by assuming an interest rate of at least 5%. Before 1983, the highest annual benefit which could have been paid by a defined-benefit pension plan was the lower of $136,425 or 100% of an employee's average pay for the highest three consecutive calendar years he or she was an active participant. The $136,425 dollar limitation included a cost-of-living adjustment.

You may not deduct more than the amount of contributions needed to fund the annual benefit under the $90,000/100% of average pay ceiling. However, those who were already accruing benefits in excess of $90,000 before 1983 will not be adversely affected; they may continue to apply the old $136,425 limit. Plan amendments reflecting the $90,000 limitation must be made by the last day of the first plan year beginning after December 31, 1983.

The $90,000 benefit limit for defined-benefit plans assumes retirement at age 65. If retirement occurs earlier or later than age 65, benefit limits are adjusted. The $90,000 limit for defined-benefit plans must be actuarially reduced using an interest rate of at least 5% for employees retiring before age 62 so that the benefit limit is equivalent to a $90,000 benefit beginning at age 62. For retirement benefits paid at or before age 55, the maximum dollar limit may not be less than the actuarial equivalent of a $75,000 annual benefit commencing at age 55. If retirement benefits do not begin until after age 65, the $90,000 defined-benefit limit must be actuarially increased so that it is the equivalent of a $90,000 benefit beginning at age 65.

68 IRA, KEOGH, AND OTHER RETIREMENT PLANS

Cost-of-living adjustments to the $90,000 defined-benefit limitation will not be allowed until 1988, when increases will be based on inflation in the calendar quarter beginning October 1, 1986.

Tax reform proposals would lower the $90,000 ceiling to $77,000.

Profit-sharing plan. There is no absolute restriction on benefits, but as a practical matter benefits are limited since there is a ceiling on the amount which may be contributed annually on behalf of each participating employee. In a profit-sharing plan, participating employees may also make voluntary contributions which are not forfeitable. Company contributions may be determined each year by separate action of the board of directors or by a contribution formula written in the trust agreement. Examples of contribution formulas:

1. The company agrees to contribute a flat percentage of profits.
2. The company agrees to contribute a percentage of profits above a set minimum.
3. The company agrees to increase the percentage as profits increase; 10% for the first $25,000 of profits; 20% for profits between $25,000 and $50,000; 30% for profits over $50,000.

The dollar limit for annual additions to an employee's account under a profit-sharing plan is $30,000. This $30,000 limit applies if it is less than the percentage limitation of 25% of compensation. Cost-of-living increases to the $30,000 limitation will not be allowed until 1988. Before 1983, the maximum amount which could have been contributed annually to an employee's profit-sharing account was the lower of 25% of compensation or $45,475, which included a cost-of-living adjustment.

The following amounts are subject to the $30,000/25% pay ceiling: employer contributions, forfeitures credited to the employee, and the lesser of (1) one-half of the employee's contribution, or (2) employee contributions in excess of 6% of compensation. Employee rollovers are not included. If an employer maintains more than one plan, the $30,000/25% limit applies to the total additions to all plans.

The $30,000/25% ceiling on annual additions also applies to defined-contribution pension plans, such as money-purchase plans, which contribute a fixed amount each year, regardless of profits.

You may make deductible contributions to a profit-sharing or stock bonus plan on behalf of permanently and totally disabled employees other than officers, owners, or highly compensated individuals. Contributions are based on the employee's compensation immediately prior to becoming disabled. The contributions must be nonforfeitable to be deductible.

A tax proposal would lower the $30,000 ceiling to $25,000.

Medical benefits for retired employees. Under prior law, medical benefits paid to retired employees and their spouses or dependents were not taken into account under the contribution and benefit limitations. Under the new law, for plan years beginning after March 31, 1984, any contributions under a defined benefit plan allocable to an individual medical account are treated as an annual addition to a defined contribution plan, subject to the $30,000/25% ceiling on annual additions. This rule applies to defined benefit plans that provide sickness, accident, hospitalization, and other medical expenses from a separate account that are payable solely to a retired employee, his spouse or his dependents. If such benefits are provided by a defined benefit plan to a retired employee who is or was at any time more than a 5% owner, or to his spouse or dependents, the benefits must be payable from a separate account set up for the employee.

Multiple plans. An employer is not limited to one plan. There may be, for example, two pension plans or one pension plan and one profit-sharing plan. However, multiple plans may not be used to exceed the contribution limit. The law requires that all the plans of an employer be aggregated to test contribution limitations.

If an employer maintains two or more similar plans (e.g., two profit-sharing plans), they are treated as one plan and total contributions may not exceed the limit for one plan. If an employer maintains two or more dissimilar plans (a pension plan and a profit-sharing plan), special limitations apply. A formula is applied on a per-employee basis each year so that total contributions and benefits stay within certain limits. The formula is the total of a defined-benefit fraction and a defined-contribution fraction. These fractions are quite complex and special elections are available. The services of a retirement expert are needed to assure compliance with the aggregate limits.

Generally, the aggregate limit is the lesser of 1.4 times the compensation limits or 1.25 times the dollar limitations. There are special transitional rules for plans in existence on or before July 1, 1982 and for the last plan year of a top-heavy plan beginning before 1984.

There is a further limitation for key employees who participate in a defined-benefit plan and defined-contribution plan included in a top-heavy group. (Top-heavy plans are discussed later in this chapter.) The aggregate limit on benefits and contributions for key employees under the defined-benefit and contribution fractions will generally be the lesser of 1.4 times the compensation limits or 1.0 times the dollar limits. The 1.0 limit may be increased to the regular 1.25 limit for multiple plans if certain additional tests are satisfied.

Covering employees

An owner may not set up a qualified plan solely for personal benefit. To obtain the benefits of a retirement plan, employees must be entitled to approximately the same benefits. However, this does not mean that a $10,000-a-year employee will receive the same retirement benefits as one earning $50,000. It means only that if each has been with the company the same length of time, they are both eligible to participate in the plan.

You can require that a new employee work for a specified length of time and reach a certain age before he or she is eligible to participate in the plan. However, you may not exclude an employee who has reached age 21 if he or she has at least one year of service. If your plan provides for full and immediate vesting of an employee's benefits, an employee may be required to complete a maximum of three years of service before participating. You need not cover seasonal or part-time employees who work less than 1,000 hours during a 12-month period.

If you set up a defined-benefit pension plan you can exclude an employee who is within five years of normal retirement age (which may not be later than age 65) when his or her period of service begins. For example, an employee hired at age 62 does not have to be included in the plan. This exclusion is not considered an act of age discrimination. A plan may also provide that no benefits are to be paid a participant until the tenth anniversary of the date the period of service began. There can be no maximum age restriction for participation in a money-purchase pension plan or profit-sharing plan.

When you set up a company plan, you must notify your employees of its existence. Failure to do so disqualifies the plan. This can be done by a letter directed to all employees telling them of the adoption of the plan by the board of directors. Once employees become plan participants, further disclosure is required. For years after 1984, employees must be given notice that certain benefits may be forfeited if they die before a particular date. Within 90 days of beginning participation, employees must receive a description of the plan. Each year they must also receive a copy of the latest annual report. When an employee terminates employment, a statement concerning vested benefits must be supplied. An employee may request a statement concerning the amount of benefits and when they will vest; the request must be in writing.

Integrating a pension or profit-sharing plan with Social Security

To the extent that employees are covered by Social Security, an employer may reduce its obligation to fund their retirement benefits. By paying a part of the employees' FICA taxes, an employer is considered to have already funded part of their retirement benefits through Social Security. When setting up a company plan, you may decide whether to take into account Social Security benefits payable to employees. You do not have to consider Social Security benefits, but if you do the IRS requires that specific tests be met to assure that the combined benefits or contributions under the plan and Social Security do not discriminate in favor of officers, stockholders, or highly paid employees. The integration rules are complex and depend on whether the company plan is a defined-benefit plan or a defined-contribution plan. These rules are set out in Treasury regulations and rulings. For example, a defined-benefit company plan may be an "offset plan" in which the total benefits called for under the plan are offset by the employees' Social Security benefits. A defined-benefit plan may be an "excess plan" in which company benefits are based only on income above a specified level. Treasury rules provide special tables for integrating such plans with Social Security.

Defined-contribution plans, such as profit-sharing plans and money-purchase pension plans, may also be integrated with Social Security by taking into account contributions rather than benefits. Here, too, rules for determining the integration level and company contributions are in Treasury regulations.

For plan years beginning after December 31, 1983, company contributions may be reduced by no more than the employer tax rate for old-age, survivors, and disability insurance (OASDI). The exact figures will depend on the Social Security wage base and OASDI tax rate for the particular year. Consider this example: Based on the 1986 employer's tax rate of 5.7% for OASDI benefits and the 1986 wage base of $42,000, a profit-sharing plan could provide no contributions for the first $42,000 of pay and make contributions equal to 5.7% of pay in excess of $42,000. If an employer wants to contribute 10% of pay over $42,000, contributions of at least 4.3% (10% − 5.7%) would have to be made for the first $42,000 in order to integrate the plan with Social Security. The OASDI rate for 1984 through 1987 is 5.7%.

When employee benefits must vest

For a qualified plan, the law imposes vesting rules to ensure that, at a definite time, all or part of an employee's benefits become nonforfeitable. A plan may adopt one of three vesting schedules:

1. 100% vesting after ten years;
2. 25% vesting after five years, 5% each year thereafter, up to 50% after ten years, and 10% each year thereafter, up to 100% after 15 years; or
3. Rule of 45, which requires that an employee's benefits must be 50% vested when his or her age and years of service together total 45 or after ten years of service, whichever occurs

first with an additional 10% vesting for each additional year of service thereafter.

The IRS may require vesting over a shorter period if faster vesting is needed to prevent discrimination in favor of officers, stockholders, and highly paid employees.

The minimum vesting schedules apply to both pension and profit-sharing plans.

Regardless of the rule used, retirement benefits from employer contributions must be at least 50% vested when the employee has ten years of service.

For plan years beginning after 1984, all years of service completed after age 18 must be taken into account in determining an employee's vested benefit.

New break-in-service rules protect nonvested employees against the loss of service credits after a break in service. Generally, an employee must be credited for years of service before the break unless the break equals or exceeds the greater of five consecutive one-year breaks or the total years of service before the break. Thus, an employee who leaves his company but returns within five years must be credited for all prior years of service. These break-in-service rules generally apply in plan years beginning after 1984, but under a transition rule, years of service may be disregarded if they did not have to be counted under the prior law minimum participation and vesting rules in effect before the first day of the first plan year beginning after 1984.

Vesting rules for top-heavy plans. For years in which a plan is top heavy as explained in the following pages, one of two vesting schedules will have to be met: (1) employees with three years of service have a nonforfeitable right to 100% of their accrued benefits from employer contributions, or (2) employee benefits are 100% vested after six years under a graded vesting schedule based on years of service, as follows:

Years of service	Amount vested
2	20%
3	40%
4	60%
5	80%
6 and more	100%

Benefits under top-heavy plans

Starting in 1984 plans (except governmental plans) that disproportionately favor owners and other key employees are subject to special rules to protect all employees in the plan. Such plans are called top-heavy plans.

A profit-sharing or other defined-contribution plan will be considered a top-heavy plan for the plan year if the account balances for "key employees" exceed 60% of the account balances for all employees. A defined-benefit plan will be considered a top-heavy plan for a plan year if the present value of the accrued benefits for "key employees" exceeds 60% of the value of the total accrued benefits for all employees. Whether a plan is top heavy is a determination made each year. The determination date is the last day of the preceding plan year (or in the case of a new plan, the last day of the first plan year). In figuring an employee's account, distributions within five years of the determination date are taken into account. Distributions from a terminated plan within the five-year period are included if the plan would have had to be included in an aggregation group of the employer if the plan had not terminated. However, a rollover contribution after 1983 is not figured into the employee's account unless the rollover was between plans of the same employer. In plan years beginning after 1984, amounts contributed on behalf of a key employee under a salary reduction arrangement must be taken into account. Further, accrued benefits of an individual are not taken into account if he has not received any compensation as an employee from the employer maintaining the plan at any time during the five-year period.

Key employees include officers (up to 50) having an annual compensation greater than 150 percent of the dollar limitation on annual additions to a defined contribution plan (currently $30,000), a more than 5% owner, a more than 1% owner with compensation over $150,000, and employees with the 10 largest ownership interests with pay exceeding the limitation on annual additions to a defined contribution plan (currently $30,000). If two employees have the same interest in the company, the one having the greater compensation will be treated as having the larger interest. Further, an individual who was an officer or owner as just described within the four preceding years is considered a key employee. Stock owned by family members will be attributed to employees under the constructive ownership rules.

If a single employer has more than one plan covering key employees, the top-heavy rules apply to the aggregated group. Plans of related employers may also be aggregated under this test.

If a plan is top heavy under the above rules it will be able to take into account only the first $200,000 of employee compensation in determining contributions or benefits. Further, there is a special limitation on the aggregate contributions and benefits for key employees under multiple plans, as noted above.

Top-heavy plans will have to provide minimum contributions or benefits to employees who are not key employees. Generally, the minimum benefit under a defined-benefit plan will be the lesser of (1) 2% of average pay in the five highest consecutive earning years times years of service, or (2) 20% of such average pay. In figuring minimum benefits, years of service completed in plan years beginning before 1984 are disregarded; also disregarded are years of service in years for which plans are not top heavy. For a defined-contribution plan, the minimum contribution for nonkey employees would generally be 3% of compensation or, if lower, the contribution rate for the highest paid key employee would apply. Social Security benefits may not be taken into account in figuring required minimum benefits or contributions.

Distributions to key employees. A 10% premature withdrawal penalty applies to distributions in 1985 to more than 5% owners whether or not the plan is top heavy. The penalty does not apply to distributions made because of the employee's disability or death. Further, individuals who own more than a 5% interest must start to receive retirement distributions by April 1 of the calendar year following the calendar year in which they reach age 70½, even if they do not retire. This rule applies to persons who own more than 5% of the stock or voting power of a corporate employer or more than 5% of the capital or profit interest of a noncorporate employer. In plan years beginning after 1983 but before 1985, plans were required to begin retirement distributions to key employees by the end of the year in which they reached age 70½, whether or not they retired.

Note: Both the premature withdrawal penalty and the beginning date for distributions after 1985 may be changed by new tax law proposals.

How much is deductible?

The corporation may claim a tax deduction for its contributions. The maximum amount of the deduction is determined by the type of plan it has set up. Limitations vary between pension or profit-sharing plans.

If your company uses an insurance company with which to fund your pension plan, it may deduct premiums charged by the insurance company which are based on reasonable actuarial assumptions and on a rigid premium structure. The premiums must be paid to the insurance company directly or through a trust; the benefits must not anticipate future increases in compensation.

Profit-sharing plan. The basic limitation on deductions to a profit-sharing plan or trust for a taxable year is 15% of the annual compensation of the covered employees. If the amount contributed to the plan is more than the deductible amount (15% of compensation), a contribution carryover is allowed. The excess contributions are deductible only in a later year when contributions are less than that year's 15% limitation. The carryover may be added to current contributions to meet the 15% ceiling, but a deduction in excess of the 15% ceiling is not allowed.

Special rules apply if contributions in one taxable year are less than the 15% deductible limit but contributions in some succeeding taxable year exceed the 15% ceiling. A credit carryover allows part or all of the unused deduction to be used in the later year when contributions exceed the 15% limit, subject to certain restrictions. In the later year and in all subsequent years in which current contributions plus contribution carryovers exceed the 15% limit, the plan's total deduction is equal to the lesser of:

1. 25% of compensation for the later year, or
2. The excess of the combined 15% limits for the year and all prior years over the total deductions allowable for all prior years.

The purpose of the above deduction formula is to produce deductions over a period of years that average 15% of compensation.

When a company contribution is made after the time allowed, the company may claim a credit carryover in a later year.

Keep in mind that profit-sharing contributions must stay within the $30,000/25% limitations on annual additions to employee accounts. If these limits are exceeded, the plan could be disqualified and no deductions would be allowed.

Defined-benefit pension plans. Generally, the maximum deductible contribution is the amount necessary to fund current plan liabilities and amortize past service costs determined actuarially. This maximum deduction applies only if it allows a greater deduction than that determined under a level cost method or normal cost method detailed in the law. A deduction may not be claimed for benefits which exceed those allowed under the $90,000/100% of average pay limit for defined-benefit plans. Anticipated cost-of-living increases may not be taken into account.

Defined-contribution pension plans. A company may deduct its contributions to a money-purchase plan (fixed contributions, regardless of profits) up to the limit for annual additions to an employee's account: 25% of compensation or $30,000. If the plan exceeds the annual addition ceilings, the plan could be disqualified and no deduction allowed.

Deduction for multiple plans. If contributions are made to more than one profit-sharing plan, the total deduction is limited to 15% of the covered employee's compensation. If contributions are made to more than one pension plan, each plan is subject to the deduction rules based on funding costs (see above). If employees are covered by both a defined-benefit pension plan and a profit-sharing plan, the deduction for each plan is limited as discussed above and, in addition, there is an overall limitation. The total deduction may not exceed the greater of 25% of employee compensation or the contribution needed for minimum funding of the pension plan; any excess is deductible in subsequent years subject to the same limitation.

When deductions are claimed

Your company claims a deduction in the year the contribution is made. However, the company may deduct a contribution made within the period ending on the due date for filing the return for that taxable year (including extensions of time).

EXAMPLES—

1. Your corporation reports on a calendar year basis. For 1986 it may deduct a contribution made any time on or before March 15, 1987—the date a calendar-year corporation must file its return.
2. Your corporation receives a two-month extension until May 15, 1987. A payment made on or before May 15, 1987, is deductible on the 1986 tax return.
3. Your corporation has a fiscal year ending June 30, 1986. Its return is due September 15, 1986. It may make a deductible contribution for the 1986 fiscal year on or before September 15, 1986.

Important: In order to claim a deduction you must set up the trust for the plan before the close of the taxable year in which the plan is to be effective.

When benefits are paid

A plan may allow for early retirement if certain service requirements are met. If a plan permits a currently employed person who has satisfied a service requirement to elect an early-retirement benefit, it must allow a past employee the same right to receive benefit payments on an actuarily reduced basis. For example, if the plan provides a monthly benefit of $100 at age 55 for those currently employed and with 30 years of service, a terminated employee who had completed 30 years of service when he or she quit at age 50 could receive a monthly benefit beginning at age 55. The benefit would be actuarially reduced.

Benefits must generally begin to be paid no later than 60 days after the close of the plan year in which the last of these events occurs:

1. The employee reaches age 65 or an earlier normal retirement age.
2. The employee completes 10 years of plan participation.
3. The employee terminates employment.

An employee may elect to delay the receipt of benefits beyond 60 days. However, even if the election is made, mandatory age distribution rules require distributions in plan years starting after 1984 to begin by April 1 of the calendar year following the later of the calendar year in which the employee reaches age 70½ or in which he retires. The entire interest must be distributed by that date or payments must begin on that date and be spread over the employee's life expectancy or the life expectancies of the employee and a designated beneficiary.

Distributions to owner-employees with more than a 5% interest must begin by April 1 of the calendar year following the calendar year in which he reaches age 70½, whether or not he retires.

Note: The above rules concerning the beginning date for retirement distributions might be changed in 1986 by new tax legislation.

If an employee starts to receive benefits but dies before his entire interest is distributed, the balance must be distributed to his beneficiaries at least as rapidly as under the method of distribution in effect before his death. If the distributions had not begun before death, his entire interest must generally be distributed within five years after his death. However, the five-year rule does not apply if the employer's interest is payable to a designated beneficiary over the beneficiary's life or over a period not extending beyond the beneficiary's life expectancy, provided distributions begin no later than one year after the date of the employee's death. The five-year rule also does not apply if the employee's interest is payable to the surviving spouse. Payments may be made under a qualified joint and survivor annuity or, starting on the date the employee would have reached age 70½, the surviving spouse starts to receive payments over his or her life or over a period not extending beyond life expectancy. If the surviving spouse is the designated beneficiary but dies before payments are to begin, then the above rules apply as if the surviving spouse were the employee.

Life expectancies of the employee or his spouse may be redetermined annually. Any amount paid to a child is treated as if paid to the surviving spouse if the amount will become payable to the spouse upon the child's majority or other designated event permitted by the regulations.

For plans under collective bargaining agreements ratified on or before July 18, 1984, the above distribution rules will not apply until the earlier of the year in which the last collective bargaining agreement relating to the plan terminates or January 1, 1988. Extensions of the agreements are disregarded. However, amendments made to the plan solely to conform to the requirements added by the new law will not be considered a termination of the agreement.

Joint and survivor annuity for spouse generally required. For plan years beginning after 1984, all defined benefit plans and money purchase plans are required to provide annuity benefits for surviving spouses. Profit-sharing or stock bonus plans must also provide automatic survivor coverage unless the participant does not elect a life annuity payment and the plan provides that the participant's nonforfeitable benefit is payable in full upon his death to his surviving spouse, or to another beneficiary if the spouse consents or there is no surviving spouse. These survivor annuity requirements do not apply to couples who have been married for less than one year as of the participant's annuity starting date, or, if earlier, the date of the participant's death.

Benefits to vested retired participants must be in the form of qualified joint and survivor annuities and in the form of qualified preretirement survivor annuities to the surviving spouses of vested participants who die before the annuity starting date. The plan must allow an employee to elect to waive such survivor benefits, but a waiver may be made only with the written consent of the spouse. An election to waive the qualified joint and survivor annuity may be made during the 90-day period ending on the annuity starting date. An election to waive the qualified preretirement survivor annuity may be made from the first day of the plan year in which the participant reaches age 35, or earlier if the participant separates from service, until the date of his death. The waiver is revocable during the time permitted to make the election.

If the present value of a qualified joint and survivor annuity or preretirement survivor annuity is $3,500 or less, the plan may distribute the account in cash prior to the annuity starting date without the consent of the participant or spouse. If the present value exceeds $3,500, written consent of the participant and his or her spouse is required for a cash-out of the annuity.

How benefits from qualified company plans are taxed

The method of payment determines how benefits are taxed. Special tax benefits are given a lump-sum distribution from a qualified plan. You may apply the ten-year averaging method for the entire distribution. Alternatively, you may avoid immediate taxation by making a tax-free rollover of all or part of your lump-sum distribution to another qualified plan or individual retirement account. If you receive your benefits as an annuity, you are taxed at ordinary income rates on the part of the payment attributable to employer contributions.

To qualify a lump-sum distribution for ten-year averaging, you must receive all that is due you under the plan. A distribution of part of your account is not a lump-sum distribution. The payment or payments must be made within one of your taxable years (usually a calendar year). The distribution must be made because you are separated from service or have reached the age of 59½, became disabled, or died. When you reach age 59½, you may receive a lump sum qualifying for special tax treatment even if you continue to work. Finally, you must be in the plan for at least five years.

If you die before collecting from the plan, your beneficiary does not have to meet the five-year test. He or she may elect ten-year averaging even if you die before age 59½.

The ten-year averaging rule for 1985 is discussed in greater detail in Chapter 7, and rollovers are discussed in Chapter 8.

Nondeductible employee contributions may be withdrawn from a qualified plan without tax. However, when 85% or more of the total contributions have been made by employees to a plan, distributions or loans made after October 16, 1984 will be first considered taxable income until all of the earnings on the account have been withdrawn.

Note: Tax reform proposals that would affect distributions after 1985, including the elimination of the ten-year averaging, are discussed in the back of this book.

Obtaining plan approval

Obtaining approval from the IRS is not necessary to qualify the plan for tax benefits, but it is advisable because of the technical tests that a plan must meet. Failure to comply will disqualify the plan and bar all tax benefits.

Use of model or prototype plans offered by an institution may avoid having to obtain a determination letter.

For advance approval, a copy of the plan must be submitted to the IRS, along with Forms 5001 and 5002.

What happens to benefits when an employee terminates employment?

Benefits that are fully vested belong to an employee even if he or she quits or is fired. The plan can specify whether to pay the benefits immediately in a lump sum or freeze the benefits until the employee reaches retirement age.

A plan can require a payout of benefits if their present value is less than $3,500. This is called an involuntary cash-out. If the employee resumes employment, he can elect to put the sum back into the plan if the original cash-out was less than the present value of his accrued benefits.

Benefits paid out upon employment termination may be rolled over to an IRA or a qualified plan of a new employer if certain conditions are met.

Benefits which do not vest to an employee are forfeited if the employee quits. The benefits remain in the plan. In pension plans, forfeitures are used to reduce employer contributions. Profit-sharing plans may also use forfeitures to reduce employer

YOUR CORPORATE RETIREMENT PLAN 83

contributions, but in practice many profit-sharing plans allocate forfeitures to the accounts of the remaining employees.

If an employee dies before retirement, the forfeiture of vested benefits attributable to company contributions may be allowed; however, a surviving spouse's qualified preretirement annuity is not forfeitable. Forfeiture before retirement is not allowed if the employee chose to continue working past the normal retirement age when he or she could have selected a joint and survivor annuity.

An employee does not forfeit vested benefits by leaving to work for a competitor.

An employee's own contributions are immediately vested. Therefore, they are not subject to forfeiture under any circumstances. However, in a plan where employee contributions are required along with employer contributions, forfeiture of employer contributions may have this result: If an employee's benefit attributable to employer's contributions is less than 50% vested, that benefit is forfeitable if the employee withdraws part or all of his contributions. Under a buy-back rule, an employee can fully restore forfeited benefits if withdrawn contributions, plus interest, are returned to the plan.

Contributions to S corporation plans

Retirement plans for S corporations are governed by the same rules applied to corporate plans. In a defined-contribution plan, contributions are generally limited to 25% of compensation or $30,000; in a defined-benefit plan, the amount necessary to provide retirement benefits may not exceed $90,000 or 100% of the average pay limit.

Substantial loans from company plans may be taxed

Your company plan may permit loans to employees, but there are limits on the amount that may be borrowed tax free. Loans may be taxed as a distribution under the following rules: A loan which is payable within five years is treated as a distribution only to the extent that it exceeds (when added to other outstanding loans from the plan) the lower of (1) $50,000 or (2) the greater of one-half of the present value of the employee's nonforfeitable plan benefit, or $10,000. Thus employees may borrow at least $10,000 with no tax consequences, as long as the loan is repayable within five years. However, a loan of accumulated deductible employee contributions is treated as a plan distribution regardless of the loan amount. Further, if the loan is used to buy, construct, or rehabilitate a principal residence of the employee or an employee's relative, a loan within the $50,000/$10,000 limitation is tax free even if it is not repaid within five years.

In all other cases, loans which are not payable within five years are treated as a distribution from the plan.

Note: More restrictive rules have been proposed for loans received after 1985.

The above rules do not affect loans which were outstanding on August 13, 1982 if they were extended or renegotiated after that date as long as they were repaid before August 14, 1983, and in the case of nonkey employees, if repaid before January 1, 1985. If they were not repaid by this date, they are treated as new loans on the date of renewal or renegotiation and are subject to the above limitations.

Reporting requirements

The law imposes reporting requirements to different sources: to employees, to the IRS, to the Department of Labor, and in some instances to the Pension Benefit Guaranty Corporation (PBGC). Some reports are required annually; others for specified events.

Stiff penalties are imposed on the employer or plan administrator for failure to comply with reporting requirements.

Chapter 5
SIMPLIFIED EMPLOYEE PENSION PLANS (SEPs)

WHETHER you are a sole proprietor, partner, or the owner of a closely held corporation, you may want to provide yourself and your employees with pension benefits without the complicated paperwork and administrative costs entailed in corporate or Keogh plans. As an employer you can set up a pension plan without creating a trust; your company merely prepares checks which are mailed to each employee's individual retirement account (IRA) or annuity. The plan is called a Simplified Employee Pension Plan, or SEP.

Under an SEP, your company may make deductible contributions to an IRA account set up by each employee. The employee reports the contribution as income but claims an offsetting deduction.

To establish an SEP, an employer need take only the following steps:

1. Sign Form 5305–SEP and give a copy of it to each employee (the form is not filed with the IRS).
2. Make a "written allocation formula," that is, set the percentage of salary used for making contributions for all covered employees.

A decision to set up an SEP should be based on a review of the after-tax cost of providing contributions and the advantages and disadvantages of the SEP compared with other pension plan alternatives.

How SEPs compare with other plans

An SEP is a pension alternative for either an incorporated or an unincorporated business. A corporation can have either a qualified pension or profit-sharing or other similar plan and/or an SEP; an unincorporated business can have a Keogh plan and/or an SEP.

The chief advantage of an SEP over other alternatives is simplicity. No formal plans or trusts are required. No special plan approval is necessary. All that is required is the written allocation formula and completion of Form 5305–SEP which is a half-page form filled out by the employer. The allocation formula is not part of the form; only the company's name, plan participation requirements, and employer's signature are needed. The form is considered properly executed when all eligible employees have set up IRAs and copies of the completed form have been given to all employees. The form is not sent to the IRS.

Further, annual reporting is greatly simplified. Thus beyond contribution costs, the cost of maintaining an SEP is virtually minimal.

While SEPs offer an employer the opportunity to set up a pension plan for a minimal expense and with greatly simplified reporting requirements, there are disadvantages. Lump-sum distributions from SEP–IRAs do not qualify for ten-year averaging. All distributions are fully taxable as ordinary income.

Another problem exists for employers who chose an SEP. The participation rule requires that all employees (with the exception of those whose earnings are $200 or less per year, certain union employees, and nonresident aliens) who are at least 25 years old and have performed service during at least three of the immediately preceding five calendar years must have contributions made to their accounts if the employer chooses to make any contributions for the year. Even the accounts of employees who have died or left the employer during the year for whatever reason must receive a contribution. For example, an employee who is otherwise eligible to participate quits in July. When contributions are made in December, the employee must receive his allocable share. Failure to give the employee his share could disqualify the entire plan. If the employee did not

SIMPLIFIED EMPLOYEE PENSION PLANS (SEPs)

establish an SEP–IRA or closed it prior to the time contributions are made, the employer must set up an IRA on the employee's behalf. The employer must send notice of the contribution in person or to the last known address of such employee. Additionally, the employer must keep a record of the payments and the institution where the employee's account is maintained.

The SEP participation rules differ from corporate and Keogh plans which focus on years of completed service. In a corporate plan for years beginning after 1984, an employee who is 21 years old must be covered if one year of service has been completed. (A three-year rule may apply in certain plans.) A year of service is defined as at least 1,000 hours in a 12-month period. Thus certain part-time employees can be excluded. Similarly, Keogh plans can exclude part-time employees. In an SEP, except for those earning below $200, all employees who have reached 25 years of age and have worked in three of the preceding five years, including part-timers, must be covered.

While the limitation on deductible contributions is the same for SEPs and Keogh or corporate plans, Keogh and corporate plans offer this advantage over an SEP: voluntary contributions may be made. While not deductible, the income earned on such contributions may accumulate tax free.

Limits on SEP contributions

The maximum deductible contribution is the lower of 15% of compensation or $30,000. Contributions must be made under a written allocation formula and bear a uniform relationship to the total compensation (not in excess of $200,000) of each employee. For example, an allocation formula calling for contributions of 10% of compensation is acceptable. A contribution rate which decreases as compensation increases is considered uniform. To illustrate, an allocation formula may call for a contribution based on 7.5% of an employee's first $10,000 of compensation and 5% of all compensation over $10,000. For purposes of these rules, a self-employed individual's compensation is earned income reduced by the deductible contribution.

Starting with plan years beginning after 1983, an SEP that is top heavy must make minimum contributions on behalf of nonkey employees under the top heavy plan rules discussed in Chapter 4.

The allocation formula does not commit an employer to make contributions annually. Contributions remain discretionary and can be made one year and not another, without regard to profits or any other criteria. Thus if you have a good year you may make contributions, but are not forced to do so if you have a bad year.

Contributions may not discriminate in favor of employees who are officers, shareholders who owned more than 10% of the value of the employer's stock, self-employed individuals, or highly compensated employees. Contributions are deemed discriminatory unless they bear a uniform relationship to the total compensation of each employee with an SEP. The percentage for figuring the contribution must generally be the same. Only the first $200,000 of compensation is taken into account. Compensation means wages, salaries, professional fees, and other amounts received for services actually rendered but does not include amounts excludable from gross income (e.g., foreign earned income).

An employer makes contributions to an employee's individual retirement account or individual retirement annuity. The model SEP provides that the employer pay contributions to each employee's IRA trustee, custodian, or insurance company (in the case of an annuity contract). The employee must set up the SEP with a bank, insurance company, or other qualified institution; the employer merely pays the contribution.

An employer is allowed to count as an employer contribution its payment of Social Security Old-Age, Survivors and Disability Insurance Contributions (OASDI) on behalf of employees, provided that such OASDI contributions are taken into account with respect to each employee maintaining an SEP. This reduces the employer's cost. The treatment of OASDI as an employer contribution is called integration. Integration may result in a lower effective rate of contribution for lower paid employees than for higher paid employees but this discrepancy is not considered discriminatory. The IRS has not yet provided a vehicle for implementing integration with OASDI. The model SEP, Form 5305–SEP, may *not* be used for plans integrated with or offset by employer OASDI payments; the model may only be used for nonintegrated plans. Also, if the plan is integrated with Social Security, the maximum contribution of $30,000 for shareholder-employees and owner-employees must be reduced by OASDI and self-employment taxes. At the time this book went to press, the maximum contribution in an integrated plan had not been set.

If your employer has an SEP

From an employee's perspective, an SEP is just like an IRA. The investment vehicle, an account with a bank or other financial institution or an annuity from an insurance company, may be left to the employee's discretion. Employees may choose different investment vehicles or different companies offering the same type of investments. Employers may wish to encourage the use of the same bank for IRA accounts by all employees for the sake of convenience in checking on the establishment of accounts by all eligible employees and in making contributions, but this cannot be required. The establishment of an IRA may be a condition of employment.

Employees may use existing IRAs, provided the bank or other trustee or custodian amends the terms of the account to accept contributions up to $30,000, since regular IRA sponsors may not accept contributions in excess of $2,000 other than rollovers.

An employer's contribution under an SEP has no effect on an employee's personal IRA contribution. Thus regardless of the amount the employer contributes, the employee may contribute up to $2,000 annually to an IRA. The maximum total deduction on the employee's return is $32,000 ($30,000 for the SEP and $2,000 for the IRA). An employee aged 70½ may claim a deduction for an SEP contribution even though a contribution to an IRA is barred.

The amount of the employer's contribution is included in the gross income figure reported on the employee's Form W-2. However, the form also separately identifies the contribution so the employee may claim the amount as an offsetting deduction. If the employer makes a contribution after the close of the calendar year, an amended W-2 must be issued to the employee.

All employee benefits are 100% vested, and there can be no prohibitions against withdrawals.

How SEP benefits are taxed

The employee with an SEP is subject to the same income tax treatment imposed on regular IRAs. SEP distributions are taxed at ordinary income rates and do not qualify for special tax treatment.

SEPs may be rolled over to other IRA investment vehicles. As with regular IRAs no more than one rollover may be made within the year, but direct transfers between trustees do not constitute rollovers.

SEPs are subject to the same penalties imposed on regular IRAs. Thus the funds must generally remain in the account until age 59½; premature withdrawals are costly.

Reporting rules

Congress created the SEP to provide a pension vehicle with minimal reporting requirements. The employer's only reporting requirement is to show the contribution on the employee's Form W-2. This must be done by January 31 of the year following the year of contribution, or 30 days after the contribution was made, whichever is later. Thus a 1985 contribution made in November is reported on the employee's W-2, which is supplied by the end of January. If a 1985 contribution is made on February 1, 1986, an amended W-2 should be supplied by March 1, 1986.

Chapter 6
DEFERRED PAY PLANS FOR INCREASED RETIREMENT BENEFITS

IF your company has a profit-sharing or stock bonus plan, it may give you the opportunity to shelter additional pay from tax. The tax law permits the company to add a cash or deferred-pay arrangement, also called a salary-reduction or 401 (K) plan, to its existing plan.

The cash or deferred-pay plan works in one of two ways:

1. Your employer contributes an amount for your benefit to a trust account. You are not taxed on your employer's contribution.
2. You agree to take a salary reduction or to forgo a salary increase. An amount equal to the pay reduction is placed in a trust account for your benefit. The reduction is treated as your employer's contribution.

Income earned on the trust account accumulates tax free until it is withdrawn. At withdrawal, the tax on the proceeds may be entitled to special averaging. This method is explained in detail in Chapter 7.

There are restrictions on when benefits can be withdrawn. You may not withdraw funds until you reach age 59½, retire, are separated from service (resign or are fired), become disabled or show financial hardship. Each plan may define financial hardship. Payments at death are not restricted.

Certain "pre-ERISA" money purchase plans (defined contribution plans) in existence on June 27, 1974 are subject to the same rules as profit-sharing or stock bonus plans with cash or deferred arrangements. These are plans that included a salary reduction arrangement as of June 27, 1974 and that provide that neither employee nor employer contributions may exceed the contribution limits in effect as of that date. Distributions from such pre-ERISA plans may *not* be made at age 59½ or on account of financial hardship, although such payments are allowed under a cash or deferred profit sharing or stock bonus plan.

Important: The new tax law proposals would sharply cut back tax advantages of 401(k) plans.

Should you take a salary reduction?

Taking a pay reduction may be an ideal way to defer income, benefit from a tax-free buildup of income, and take advantage of ten-year averaging at distribution. In the past, if salary was under the base for Social Security taxes, a reduction in salary could have reduced future Social Security benefits because salary reductions were not subject to Social Security (FICA) or other payroll taxes. Salary reductions under deferred pay plans are subject to FICA and FUTA withholdings.

Participating in a deferred-pay or salary-reduction plan does not prevent you from also contributing to an IRA account. However, if your investment dollars are limited and you must choose between setting up your own IRA or contributing to a salary-reduction plan, consider the relative merits of each plan.

With an IRA, you must take the initiative to seek out an investment, such as a bank CD or an annuity. Further, you must meet your contribution obligation yourself. With a salary reduction plan, you have to do nothing more than consent. The plan is set up and administered by your company plan's trustees. Contributions are automatic; they are withheld from your pay and transferred to the plan.

The maximum salary reduction contribution is not a fixed dollar amount but rather a percentage of compensation. Salary reductions are treated as employer contributions. If total company retirement plan contributions are limited to 15% of compensation and the company contributes 10% to a profit-sharing plan, the limitation on an employee's salary reduction would be 5%. If the company plans to match employee contributions, the salary reduction limitation would be 2½%. This means that workers with greater earnings will be able to contribute more to the plan than workers with smaller earnings. Assume a plan permits salary reduction up to 5% of compensation. For workers earning less than $40,000, contributions would be below the amount that could be put into an IRA; for those earning above $40,000, contributions to a salary-reduction plan would outstrip IRA contributions. For example, an executive earning $60,000 could contribute $2,000 to an IRA. That same executive could have his or her salary reduced by 5% or $3,000 and have that money contributed to the company's plan.

The current tax saving for an equal amount of money put into an IRA or into a salary-reduction plan is the same.

Cash or deferred-pay plan may not discriminate

For a plan to qualify, it must not discriminate in favor of highly compensated employees. To judge whether there is discrimination, there are two tests, a coverage test, and a contribution percentage test. Under the coverage test, the plan must benefit either (1) 70% or more of all employees or 80% or more of all eligible employees if 70% or more are eligible, or (2) employees that qualify under a classification set up by the employer which is found by the Secretary not to be discriminatory.

Under the contribution percentage tests, employees are grouped into a higher paid one third and a lower paid two thirds. One of two percentage tests must be satisfied: (1) the average percentage of pay contributed by the higher paid one-third group is not more than 1½ times the average percent of pay contributed by the lower paid two-thirds, or (2) the average percentage contribution for the top one-third group is no more than 3% greater than the average percentage contribution for the lower two-thirds. The average percentage contribution for the top one-third must also be no more than 2½ times the average percentage for the lower two-thirds. Thus if the lower paid group deferred an average 2% of their pay, the upper one-third group could average as much as 5% deferral without creating a discrimination problem. If two or more plans are considered as one plan for purposes of meeting the general nondiscriminatory requirements for qualified plans, then the cash or deferred arrangements of the plans will be treated as one arrangement for purposes of applying the above contribution percentage tests which are specifically applicable to cash or deferred arrangements. Furthermore, if an employee is a participant in two or more cash or deferred arrangements of an employer, the sum of the deferral percentages under each arrangement will be the percentage taken into account for purposes of the contribution percentage tests mentioned above.

For plan years beginning after July 18, 1984, the discrimination rules discussed above apply to pre-ERISA money purchase plans as well as profit sharing and stock-bonus plans that have cash or deferred arrangements. A pre-ERISA money purchase plan is a pension plan which is a defined-contribution plan (discussed in Chapter 4) in existence on June 27, 1974, which included a salary reduction arrangement on that date, and under which neither employee nor employer contributions may exceed the plan's contribution formula limits in effect on that date.

For the employer, the discrimination issue presents a real problem. While the plan is offered to all employees, there is no way to know in advance how many and to what extent employees will take up the pay-reduction option. Salary reductions cannot be mandatory. What happens if an employer offers the plan but only highly paid employees decide to defer pay? The plan is disqualified and contributions are currently taxed, but plan contributions are probably still locked into the plan until employees reach age 59½. Generally, employers need not fear a discrimination problem. Where the plan has been offered, employee acceptance has been enthusiastic. When one large company offered the plan, 85% of its employees chose to participate.

How benefits are taxed. All IRA distributions, whether paid in a lump sum or periodic installments, are subject to the same tax treatment: distributions are added to your other income and taxed at ordinary income tax rates. However, distributions from salary-reduction plans may receive special tax treatment. If the distribution is paid out in a lump sum, it may qualify for special ten-year averaging. This method results in considerably lower tax on the distribution than if ordinary income tax rates applied.

DEFERRED PAY PLANS FOR INCREASED BENEFITS

Restrictions. IRA and salary-reduction plans are subject to similar restrictions in that the funds may not generally be touched until employees reach age 59½, unless they are disabled. Withdrawing money sooner incurs tax penalties. However, the salary-reduction plan allows withdrawals without a penalty prior to age 59½ if you leave the company or in the case of substantial financial hardship. However, this hardship provision (and the age 59½ allowance) does not apply to pre-ERISA money purchase plans. Exactly what substantial financial hardship means has yet to be determined. The IRS has said only that it must be "immediate and heavy." Each plan must set up a board or committee to review claimed hardships on a case-by-case basis, according to uniform and nondiscriminatory standards set forth in the plan. It has been suggested that the hardship test may be liberally construed. For example, inability to get a home mortgage at a reasonable rate may be a sufficient hardship to warrant a penalty-free distribution. There is, of course, the question of privacy and how much financial and personal disclosure the plan's committee can legally require. A statement by an employee claiming hardship may be all that is required.

Salary-reduction plans for employees of tax-exempt groups and schools

If you are employed by a tax-exempt religious, charitable, or educational organization, or if you are on the civilian staff or faculty of the Uniformed Services University of the Health Sciences (Department of Defense), you may be able to purchase a tax-deferred retirement annuity, generally through a salary reduction which pays for the contract. Salary reductions are treated as employer contributions. Contributions may be invested in mutual fund shares as well as in annuity contracts.

The amount of the salary reduction is not taxable if it comes within these rules: the tax-sheltered contribution is generally 20% of your pay multiplied by the number of years of service with your employer, less salary reductions or employer contributions to any employer qualified plan which were tax free in prior taxable years. However, a contribution may be taxable to the extent it exceeds the lesser of 25% of compensation, or the defined-contribution dollar limit of $30,000.

96 IRA, KEOGH, AND OTHER RETIREMENT PLANS

EXAMPLE—

Your salary is $20,000 and your contribution computed under the 20% rule is $4,000. Assuming that this is your first year of service, you are not taxed on the $4,000 contribution as it comes within the 20% limit: 20% of $20,000 ($20,000 × 1 year service) or $4,000. It also comes within the 25% contribution limit: 25% of $20,000, or $5,000.

Employees of schools, hospitals, and home health services may specially elect to make tax-free contributions greater than those allowed under the 25% of compensation ceiling but which fall within the general 20% of pay exclusion. Such employees may elect to exclude from pay the lowest of: (1) the general 20% of pay/years of service exclusion discussed earlier; (2) 25% of pay plus $4,000; or (3) $15,000. Once this election is made for any year, the election is irrevocable and will apply to all future years.

Employees of schools, hospitals, and home health agencies may make an irrevocable election to disregard the general 20% of pay test. If the election is made, the annual tax-free contribution equals the contribution limit for defined-contribution plans which is the lesser of 25% of pay or $30,000. Amounts paid by an employer to a tax-sheltered annuity under a salary reduction agreement are treated as part of the wage base for FICA and FUTA (after 1984) purposes.

The above contribution rules have been stated in general terms and other elections may be available, as explained in temporary Treasury regulations. You should ask your employer or the issuer of the contract to compute the maximum tax-free contribution.

Church employees. For duly ordained ministers and church lay employees with adjusted gross income of $17,000 or less (without regard to their spouse's income), tax-free contributions may be made up to the lesser of $3,000 or taxable compensation, even if this exceeds the amount otherwise allowable under the general 20% of pay/years of service test. Further, such church employees may make an election which allows contributions to be made in excess of the defined-contribution

DEFERRED PAY PLANS FOR INCREASED BENEFITS

limitation. If the election is made, contributions of up to $10,000 may be made for any one year, subject to a lifetime limitation of $40,000. Such contributions are tax free if they are within the 20% of pay exclusion.

How annuity distributions are taxed. If benefits are paid as an annuity, each installment is fully taxable if all of the contributions were tax free under the above rules. If excess contributions were taxable, you may recover this amount tax free. If benefits are in the form of a lump-sum distribution, a rollover may be made to an IRA. If you do not make a rollover, the lump sum is taxed as ordinary income; the special ten-year averaging method allowed for lump-sum distributions from qualified company plans is not available.

Chapter 7
TAX TREATMENT OF RETIREMENT BENEFITS

THE following chapter applies to distributions subject to the law effective in 1985. Proposed tax rules which may apply to benefits received in 1986 and later years is discussed in the guide to the new law proposals at the end of this book.

How to treat lump-sum distributions from qualified retirement plans

A lump-sum distribution from a qualified plan is subject to special tax rules. If you participated in a plan before 1974, contributions made before 1974 may be taxable as long-term capital gain. Part of a lump-sum distribution may be ordinary income taxable under the special ten-year averaging rule. You may even elect to apply the ten-year averaging method to the entire distribution. Alternatively, you may avoid immediate taxation by making a tax-free rollover of all or part of your lump-sum distribution to another qualified plan or an IRA. Distributions from an IRA do not qualify for capital gain treatment or ten-year averaging.

To qualify as a lump-sum distribution, these tests must be met:

1. Payment must be from a qualified pension or profit-sharing plan. A qualified plan is one approved by the IRS. A Civil Service retirement system that has a trust fund may be treated as a qualified plan. Ask your retirement plan administrator whether your plan is qualified.

2. You must receive all that is due you under the plan. A distribution of only part of your account is not a lump-sum distribution. If your employer's plan uses more than one trust, you must receive a distribution of all that is due you from each trust.

3. The payment or payments must be made within one of your taxable years (usually a calendar year). For example, you retired on October 31, 1985, and start receiving monthly annuity payments under the company's plan on November 1, 1985. On February 3, 1986, you take the balance to your credit in lieu of any future annuity payments. The payments to you do not qualify as a lump sum; you did not receive them within one taxable year. However, if you had taken the balance of your account on or before December 31, 1985, all the payments would qualify.

4. If you are an employee, the distribution must be made because you are "separated from service" (discussed later), reach the age of 59½, or die. If you are self-employed, the lump-sum distribution from your Keogh plan must be made when you reach age 59½, become disabled, or die.

An employee who has reached age 59½ may receive a lump sum qualifying for special tax treatment even if he continues to work at his position. At one time the IRS said this was true only if the distribution was from a profit-sharing plan. However, the IRS agreed to apply the favorable rule to pension plans as well, provided the employee has reached both age 59½ and the normal retirement age as defined in the company plan.

Under some plans you receive an amount attributed to your last year of work after the year in which you were paid a lump sum. This payment does not affect special treatment of the lump sum. It is treated as the receipt of ordinary income because it was not paid in the same taxable year as the lump sum.

Disqualification of retirement plan. If you receive a lump-sum distribution from a plan which loses its exempt status, the IRS may argue that the distribution does not qualify for lump-sum treatment. Under the IRS position, you may not roll over the distribution to an IRA or elect 10-year averaging. However, appeals courts split on the issue, and the Tax Court holds that if the plan qualified when contributions were made, an allocable portion of the distribution is a qualified lump sum.

EXAMPLE—

In 1977, Baetens received a $21,077 lump-sum distribution when his company terminated its profit-sharing plan. He rolled over the distribution to an IRA. In 1979, the IRS retroactively disqualified the plan for tax years ending on or after March 31, 1974. Although Baeten's company had made all of its contributions before the disqualification date, the IRS ruled that as the plan was not qualified on the date of the 1977 distribution, the distribution was not a lump sum that could be rolled over to an IRA. The Tax Court disagrees. The status of the plan at the time of contribution controls, not status on the distribution date. To hold otherwise would penalize an innocent employee who had no say in the management of the trust and retroactively change the ground rules which he thought would govern the tax treatment of his benefits.

On appeal, a federal appeals court reversed and sided with the IRS.

Capital gain and ordinary income portions are allocated. The company paying the lump-sum distribution has the responsibility of allocating the capital gain and ordinary-income portions on Form 1099R or other statement accompanying the distribution. Part of the lump-sum distribution representing the proportion of the number of years in which an employee was a member of a qualified plan before 1974 to the total number of years of participation is the capital gain portion. The balance attributed to the post-1973 participation period is taxable as ordinary income to which the ten-year averaging method may be applied.

Ten-year averaging

Tax under the ten-year averaging rule is figured separately and apart from tax on your other income and the portion of the distribution qualifying as capital gain (see below). The effect of the averaging method is to tax the ordinary-income portion of a lump-sum distribution as if it were received evenly over a ten-year period. This results in a substantially lower tax than if the distribution were included with your other income and taxed at regular income tax rates.

Ten-year averaging is computed on Form 4972 with the tax taken from the unmarried individuals' tax rate schedule (single), regardless of your marital or head-of-household status. The separate tax figured under the ten-year averaging rule is added to your regular tax. This means that you do not include the ordinary-income element in your income when you compute your regular tax. Use of ten-year averaging does not bar you from applying the regular averaging rules to your other income and capital gain.

Here are sample effective tax rates on various distributions:

Amount of distribution	Effective tax rate in: 1985
Up to $20,000	5.5%
$25,000	7.2
$30,000	8.4
$40,000	10.5
$50,000	11.8
$75,000	13.8
$100,000	14.6

You cannot use ten-year averaging unless you have been a participant in the plan for five or more years before the taxable year of the lump-sum distribution. If you receive lump-sum distributions from more than one qualified plan, you may elect the ten-year averaging method only once after you reach age 59½. Before age 59½ there is no limit to the number of times you may elect the ten-year averaging method. Filing Form 4972 acts as an election to use ten-year averaging.

If you are an employee, part of your lump-sum payment may be treated as long-term capital gain whether or not you elect ten-year averaging. That is, you will still treat part of your payment as capital gain although you participated in the plan for less than five years and therefore are not permitted to use the ten-year averaging method. Similarly, you may be barred from electing ten-year averaging because you already elected to use it once after you reached age 59½, although part of your payment may be capital gain.

If you are self-employed, part of your lump-sum distribution may be treated as capital gain only if you elect ten-year averaging. Thus you may not treat part of your payment as capital gain if you have not participated in the plan for more than five years.

If you are a beneficiary of a deceased employee, the five-year test does not apply. You may elect ten-year averaging whether or not the employee was a participant in the plan for more than five years. Further, you may elect ten-year averaging if the employee had not reached age 59½. However, if the employee was 59½ or older, you may elect ten-year averaging only once with respect to distributions you receive as his beneficiary. A lump-sum payment to you on account of the employee's death may qualify for capital gain and ten-year averaging treatment, although the employee received annuity payments before he died.

If you receive a lump-sum distribution but do not satisfy the five-year participation rule, you may not use ten-year averaging, but you may make a tax-free rollover to defer tax on the payment.

Election to treat capital gain as ordinary income. On Form 1099R your company lists the capital gain and ordinary-income elements of the distribution. You may want to elect to treat the entire lump-sum distribution from a qualified plan as ordinary income. In most situations the effective tax rate of ten-year averaging is less than the effective capital gain rate. This may be checked by computing the tax under both methods. The election is also advisable if you will be subject to alternative minimum tax on the capital gains portion. The election to treat the entire sum as ordinary income is made on Form 4972 simply by entering the entire distribution as ordinary income.

The election is irrevocable. Once you make it, all later lump-sum distributions from other qualified plans are treated as ordinary income. But you may not make this special election if after 1975 you received a lump-sum distribution and treated the pre-1974 element as long-term capital gain.

If you receive a lump-sum distribution as a beneficiary of a deceased employee, you may make the ordinary-income election; all later lump-sum distributions you receive as beneficiary of the same employee must also be treated as ordinary income. If you received a lump-sum distribution as beneficiary and treated the pre-1974 element as capital gain, you may not make this special election for any other lump sums you receive as beneficiary of the same employee.

The taxable portion of a lump-sum distribution does not include the employee's contributions to the plan and net un-

TAX TREATMENT OF RETIREMENT BENEFITS

realized appreciation on a distribution of securities of the employer.

EXAMPLE—

An employee receives a lump-sum distribution of $65,000 including stock of his employer. The stock had a basis of $10,000 when put in the plan; it is valued at $25,000 when distributed, resulting in a net unrealized appreciation of $15,000. The employee did not contribute to the plan. The taxable portion of the distribution is $50,000 ($65,000 − $15,000). The $50,000 is then allocated between the capital gain and ordinary income portions.

Community property. Only the spouse who has earned the lump-sum distribution may apply the ten-year averaging method. Community-property laws are disregarded for purposes of computing this tax. If a couple filed separate returns and one spouse elects the ten-year averaging method, the other spouse is not taxable on the amount subject to the computation.

EXAMPLE—

A husband in a community-property state receives a lump-sum distribution of which the ordinary-income portion is $10,000. He and his wife file separate returns. If the ten-year averaging computation is not elected, $5,000, or one-half, is taxable in the husband's return and the other $5,000 in his wife's return. However, if he elects the ten-year averaging method, only he reports the $10,000 on Form 4972.

Look-back rule for annuity contracts or receipt of more than one lump sum during a six-year period. The use of the ten-year averaging method is modified by a "look-back" provision which requires that the lump-sum distributions for the taxable year be aggregated with all post-1973 lump-sum distributions made during the five previous tax years. This increases the bracket at which the ordinary-income portion of the current year's lump-sum distribution is taxed. You do not aggregate lump sums paid before 1974 or post-1973 lump sums which were not subject to the ten-year averaging rule.

A look-back rule is also applied to the distribution of an

annuity contract, although its total value is not taxable when distributed. The current actuarial value is included in the six-year aggregation computation to determine the taxable bracket of the ordinary income portion of a current lump-sum distribution. An example of computing tax when a distribution includes an annuity contract is in the instructions accompanying Form 4972.

Separation-from-service test for employees

Employees who have not reached the age of 59½ must be separated from service to be eligible for the favorable tax treatments accorded distributions. The separation-from-service test requires that you have retired, resigned, or have been discharged. If a plan is terminated but you continue working, distributions are not entitled to special lump-sum treatment if you have not reached age 59½. After you reach age 59½ the separation-from-service test need not be met. According to the IRS, if you receive a lump-sum distribution from a pension plan after age 59½ and continue working you also must have reached the normal retirement age as fixed in the company plan to qualify for special tax treatment, unless the plan was terminated.

The separation-from-service test generally prevents lump-sum treatment when a qualified plan is terminated following a reorganization or merger of a company. According to the IRS, an employee under age 59½ receiving a lump-sum distribution from the plan may not claim lump-sum treatment. This IRS position is a reversal of a prior policy under which lump-sum treatment was sometimes permitted. Under the current IRS position, payments following reorganization, liquidation, or merger are not considered lump-sum payments to employees remaining with the successor corporation. In one case, however, an appeals court held that a beneficial change in ownership and eventual liquidation of the employer corporation resulted in the employee's "separation from service." Similarly, in a private letter ruling, the IRS said that separation from service had occurred where employees had been effectively terminated before being hired in new capacities by the company that bought out their old firm.

TAX TREATMENT OF RETIREMENT BENEFITS

Important: A lump sum paid on account of termination of a plan may be rolled over tax free to an IRA.

Partnership plans. Lump-sum payments made on the termination of a plan when a partnership dissolves do not qualify for special lump-sum treatment when the employees continue to work for the successor partnership. Similarly, an employee of a partnership who becomes a partner and has to quit the firm's employee profit-sharing plan may not treat the payment as a lump sum. He or she is still serving the firm.

Lump-sum payments received by beneficiary

A beneficiary of a deceased employee may apply the special lump-sum rules to a payment received because of the employee's death. In addition, the $5,000 death benefit exclusion may also be claimed. The $5,000 exclusion for payments to beneficiaries also applies in the case of self-employed owners who die after 1983. Any federal estate tax attributable to the distribution is deductible.

A beneficiary may elect to forgo the favorable income tax treatment for lump-sum benefits in order to reduce the estate tax on the distribution. Whether it is advisable to make this election is discussed in Chapter 10.

Payment received by a second beneficiary (after the death of the first beneficiary) is not entitled to lump-sum treatment or the death-benefit exclusion.

EXAMPLES—

1. Gunnison's father was covered by a company benefit plan. The father died, as did his widow, before benefits were fully paid out. Gunnison received a substantial lump sum and argued that he should be eligible to use lump-sum treatment because he collected benefits on account of his father's death. The IRS disagreed. The Tax Court and an appeals court sided with the IRS. Gunnison was entitled to the payment following his mother's death, not his father's death. The payout must arise solely on account of the death of the covered employee to qualify for special lump-sum treatment.

2. Robert's employer announced the termination of the com-

pany's pension plan. Before benefits were distributed, Robert died. His widow received a lump-sum distribution as his beneficiary. After subtracting the amount attributable to Robert's contributions, she excluded $5,000 as a death benefit and treated the balance as a lump-sum distribution. The IRS claimed she received the distribution on the termination of the plan, not because of Robert's death. The Tax Court agreed. Distribution was made to her under the termination provisions, not the provisions for withdrawal due to separation from service or death. She could not take a death-benefit exclusion, and the distribution (less Robert's contributions) could not be treated as a lump-sum distribution.

Lump-sum distribution to more than one beneficiary. A lump-sum distribution to two or more individuals may qualify for capital gain treatment and the ten-year averaging method. The distribution is first treated as made to one recipient to determine whether it is a lump sum and what portion is taxable as capital gain. Each beneficiary may separately elect the ten-year averaging method for the ordinary-income portion, even if other beneficiaries do not.

Distribution to trust or estate. If a lump sum is paid to a trust or estate, the employee, or a personal representative if the employee is deceased, may elect to use the ten-year averaging method. This is true even though the ordinary-income portion is distributed to the beneficiaries in the year the lump sum was received. If the fiduciary makes the election, the ordinary income is taxable to the trust or estate even if a distribution is made to the beneficiary. However, the capital gain portion, if distributed to the beneficiaries in the year received by the trust or estate, is taxable as long-term capital gain to the beneficiaries, not to the trust. If the distribution is to the beneficiaries of a self-employed person, the beneficiaries may not treat the capital gain portion as capital gain unless the trust or estate also makes an election to use the ten-year averaging method.

Securities received as distribution

When your company plan distributes securities of the company, the amount reported as income depends on the value of

TAX TREATMENT OF RETIREMENT BENEFITS 107

the securities, the amount contributed by the company for the securities, and whether the distribution qualifies as a lump-sum payment.

Lump-sum payments. If the distribution is of appreciated securities and is part of a lump-sum distribution, the unrealized appreciation is not subject to tax at the time of distribution. Only the amount of the employer's contribution is subject to tax. Tax on the appreciation is delayed until the shares are later sold by you at a price exceeding cost basis. If, when distributed, the shares are valued at below the cost contribution of the employer, the fair market value of the shares is subject to tax. If you contributed to the purchase of the shares and their value is less than your contribution, you do not realize a loss deduction on the distribution. You realize a loss only when the stock is sold or becomes worthless at a later date. If a plan distributes worthless stock, you may deduct your contributions to the stock as an ordinary loss if you itemize deductions.

EXAMPLES—

1. Shares valued below your cost contribution. You contributed $500 and your employer contributed $300 to buy ten shares of company stock having a fair market value of $80 per share, or a total of $800. You do not realize income on the distribution, and you do not have a deductible loss for the difference between your cost contribution and the lower fair market value. Your contribution to the stock is its basis. This is $50 per share. If you sell the stock for $40 per share, you have a capital loss of $10 per share. However, if you sell the stock for $60 per share, you have gain of $10 per share.

2. Appreciated shares. You receive ten shares of company stock to which only the employer contributed toward their purchase. Your employer's cost was $50 a share. At the time of distribution the shares are valued at $80 a share. Your employer's contribution of $50 a share, or $500, is included as part of your taxable distribution. The appreciation of $300 is not included. The cost basis of the shares in your hands is $500 (the amount currently taxable to you). The holding period of the stock starts at the date of distribution. However, if you sell the shares for any amount exceeding $500 and up to $800, your profit is long-term gain even if the sale is within one year of the date of the distribution. If you sell for more than $800, the gain exceeding the original unrealized appreciation of $300 is subject to long-term capital gain treatment only if the sale is long term from the date of distribution. Thus if within a month of the distribution you sold the shares for $900, $300 would be long-term gain; $100 would be short-term gain.

Other than lump-sum payments. If you receive appreciated securities in a distribution that does not meet the lump-sum tests, you report as ordinary income the amount of the employer's contribution to the purchase of the shares and the appreciation allocated to his cost contribution. You do not report the amount of appreciation allocated to your contribution. However, a less favorable rule applies if you receive a qualifying partial distribution which you elect to roll over; *see* below.

EXAMPLE—

A qualified plan distributes ten shares of company stock with an average cost of $100, of which the employee contributed $60 and the employer $40. At the date of distribution the stock had a fair market value of $180. The portion of the unrealized appreciation attributable to the employee's contribution is $48 (60% of $80); the employer's is $32 (40% of $80). The employee reports $72 as income; the employer's cost is $40 and his or her share of appreciation is $32. The basis of each share is $132, which includes employee contribution of $60 and the $72 reported as taxable income. Net unrealized appreciation and cost contributions must be supplied by the company distributing the stock.

Rollover of partial distribution

Under prior law, a rollover of a retirement distribution could be made only if it was a lump sum. Under a new law, certain partial distributions received after July 18, 1984 from a qualified pension or profit-sharing plan, or a tax-sheltered annuity may be rolled over to an IRA. To qualify, the distribution must equal at least 50% of your plan account balance and it must

TAX TREATMENT OF RETIREMENT BENEFITS

not be one of a series of periodic payments. The IRA rollover must be made within 60 days. A rollover may not be made to another qualified plan. Under the 50% test, you may disregard amounts credited to you under other qualified plans maintained by the same employer. If you elect rollover treatment, a later distribution of your entire account balance from the plan from which you received the partial distribution will not qualify for 10-year averaging or capital gain treatment. A surviving spouse who receives a qualifying partial distribution may also make a rollover to an IRA. Further, if you receive appreciated securities as part of the partial distribution and you elect rollover treatment, you must report as income the amount of appreciation allocated to your contributions. This is an exception to the rule, discussed above, that where a distribution does not meet the lump-sum tests, you only have to report appreciation allocated to employer contributions.

How annuity payments are taxed

Retirement benefits paid as annuities are generally taxed in the same manner as commercial annuities. That is, part of the annuity payment is treated as a nontaxable return of your cost (premiums or other amounts are explained below); part is taxable income earned on your investment. But if your pension was completely financed by your employer and you did not include as income your employer's premium contributions, you report all periodic payments you receive as ordinary income. You have no cost investment in the annuity contract.

Figuring your cost factor. Cost includes the following items:

1. Premiums paid by you or by withholdings from your pay.
2. Payments made by your employer and reported as additional pay. Premiums paid by an employer in a nonapproved plan for your benefit give you immediate income if you have nonforfeitable rights to the policy.
3. Premiums paid by your employer which, if the amounts had been paid to you directly, would have been tax free to you because you were working abroad.
4. Pre-1939 contributions by a city or state to its employees'

110 IRA, KEOGH, AND OTHER RETIREMENT PLANS

pension fund. (Before 1939 salary payments to state and city employees were tax free for federal income tax purposes.)

5. If you are a beneficiary collecting because of the death of an employee, cost may include all or part of the death-benefit exclusion up to $5,000.

Three-year recovery of cost

If within three years of the first payment, payments under the contract will equal or exceed your cost investment, they are not taxable as income until after they equal your cost investment.

EXAMPLES—

1. Starting July 1, 1984, you receive a pension annuity of $300 a month for the rest of your life. You contributed $9,000 to the policy; your company paid the balance. Because payments will equal or exceed your cost within three years, payments received before January 1, 1987, are not taxable income.

Payments in	*Total*
1984 (six months)	$1,800
1985	3,600
1986	3,600
	$9,000

2. Same facts as above except you contributed only $6,000 to the policy.

Payments in	*Total*
1984 (six months)	$1,800
1985	3,600
1986 (two months)	600
	$6,000

Taxable payments (ten months) reported in 1986 total $3,000.

After you have received payments equaling your investment, all future payments are ordinary income.

TAX TREATMENT OF RETIREMENT BENEFITS

If you will not recover your cost within three years after your pension starts, follow the rules discussed below.

An increase in the amount of payments during the three-year period does not permit use of the three-year rule if you could not have used it initially.

An employee is taxed on the full value of a nonforfeitable annuity contract which his or her employer buys if the employer does not have a qualified pension plan. Tax is imposed in the year the policy is purchased.

You may receive benefits from more than one program under a single trust or plan of an employer or from several trusts or plans. Check with your former employer if you are covered by more than one pension or annuity contract. If so, you have to account for each contract separately even though benefits are included in one check.

Variable annuity. The three-year cost rules apply to periodic payments under a variable annuity contract financed by you and your employer. To determine whether you will recover your cost within three years, multiply the amount of the first periodic payment by the number of periodic payments to be made within the three years beginning on the date of its receipt.

How annuities are taxed if you cannot use the three-year rule

If you cannot use the three-year rule to report your annuity, you must follow six steps to determine which part of each payment is taxable and which part is tax free.

1. Figure your investment in the annuity, as discussed above.

2. Find your expected return. This is the total of all the payments you are to receive. If the payments are to be made to you for life, your expected return is figured by multiplying the amount of the annual payment by a multiple based on your life expectancy as of the annuity starting date. These multiples are listed in tables published by the Treasury. The tables are available from your local district director, or you can write to your insurance company, requesting the amount of your expected return. Below is the table to use when payments are made to one person for life and cease on that person's death.

Find your age at the birthday nearest your annuity starting date in the proper column—"Male" or "Female." Then look opposite your age to find the proper multiple. You then multiply this figure by the total annuity payments you are to receive in one full year. If you have a monthly annuity, you multiply the figure by 12 times the monthly payments. The product is your expected return.

If the payments are for a fixed number of years (as in an endowment contract), find your expected return by multiplying your annual payments by the number of years you are to receive them.

3. Divide the investment in contract (step 1) by the expected return (step 2). This will give you the percentage of your yearly annuity payments which is tax free. The percentage remains the same for the remaining years of the annuity.

4. Find your total annuity receipts for the year. For example, you received ten monthly payments, as your annuity began in March. Your total is the monthly payment multiplied by ten.

5. Multiply the percentage in step 3 by the total in step 4. The resulting amount is the nontaxable portion (or excludable amount) of your annuity payments.

6. Subtract the amounts in step 5 from the amount figured in step 4. This is the part of your annuity subject to tax for the year. Here is an example of how an employee who would not recover his or her cost within three years must report retirement pay:

EXAMPLE—

Jones was 66 years old on March 14, 1985. On April 1 he received his first monthly annuity check of $100 covering his payment for March. His annuity starting date is March 1, 1985. Looking at the table for a male at age 66, Jones finds the multiple 14.4. Jones multiplies 14.4 by $1,200 ($100 a month for a year) to find his expected return of $17,280. Assume the annuity cost Jones $12,960. He divides his expected return into

TAX TREATMENT OF RETIREMENT BENEFITS

Ages Male	Ages Female	Multiples	Ages Male	Ages Female	Multiples	Ages Male	Ages Female	Multiples
6	11	65.0	41	46	33.0	76	81	9.1
7	12	64.1	42	47	32.1	77	82	8.7
8	13	63.2	43	48	31.2	78	83	8.3
9	14	62.3	44	49	30.4	79	84	7.8
10	15	61.4	45	50	29.6	80	85	7.5
11	16	60.4	46	51	28.7	81	86	7.1
12	17	59.5	47	52	27.9	82	87	6.7
13	18	58.6	48	53	27.1	83	88	6.3
14	19	57.7	49	54	26.3	84	89	6.0
15	20	56.7	50	55	25.5	85	90	5.7
16	21	55.8	51	56	24.7	86	91	5.4
17	22	54.9	52	57	24.0	87	92	5.1
18	23	53.9	53	58	23.2	88	93	4.8
19	24	53.0	54	59	22.4	89	94	4.5
20	25	52.1	55	60	21.7	90	95	4.2
21	26	51.1	56	61	21.0	91	96	4.0
22	27	50.2	57	62	20.3	92	97	3.7
23	28	49.3	58	63	19.6	93	98	3.5
24	29	48.3	59	64	18.9	94	99	3.3
25	30	47.4	60	65	18.2	95	100	3.1
26	31	46.5	61	66	17.5	96	101	2.9
27	32	45.6	62	67	16.9	97	102	2.7
28	33	44.6	63	68	16.2	98	103	2.5
29	34	43.7	64	69	15.6	99	104	2.3
30	35	42.8	65	70	15.0	100	105	2.1
31	36	41.9	66	71	14.4	101	106	1.9
32	37	41.0	67	72	13.8	102	107	1.7
33	38	40.0	68	73	13.2	103	108	1.5
34	39	39.1	69	74	12.6	104	109	1.3
35	40	38.2	70	75	12.1	105	110	1.2
36	41	37.3	71	76	11.6	106	111	1.0
37	42	36.5	72	77	11.0	107	112	.8
38	43	35.6	73	78	10.5	108	113	.7
39	44	34.7	74	79	10.1	109	114	.6
40	45	33.8	75	80	9.6	110	115	.5
						111	116	0

the investment in the contract (the cost) and determines his exclusion percentage, 75%. Thereafter, in every year for the rest of his life, Jones receives 75% of his annuity payments tax free and is taxed on 25%. For 1985 Jones reports his annuity income as follows:

Amount received	$900
Amount excludable	675
Taxable portion	$225

For 1986 and later years Jones will receive annuity payments for the full year. The amount received will be $1,200; the amount excludable is $900; the taxable portion is $300.

How Civil Service retirement pay is taxed

Almost all U.S. Civil Service retirees use the three-year rule since they usually receive annuity benefits sufficient to recover their cost within three years after they retire.

While you worked for the federal government, contributions to the Civil Service retirement fund were withheld from your pay. These contributions represent your cost. Also, if you repaid to the retirement fund amounts that you previously had withdrawn, or paid into the fund to receive full credit for certain uncovered service, the entire amount you paid, including that designated as interest, is part of your cost. You may not claim an interest deduction for any amount designated as interest.

The Civil Service annuity statement you received when your annuity was approved shows your "total contributions" to the retirement fund (your cost) and the "monthly rate" of your annuity benefit. The monthly rate is the rate before adjustment for health benefits coverage and life insurance, if any. To determine whether you will recover your cost within three years, multiply your initial monthly rate by 36. If the result equals or exceeds your cost, you must use the three-year rule. If you will not recover your cost within the three-year period, follow the six-step approach outlined above.

An increase in the monthly rate of your annuity resulting

from a cost-of-living increase does not affect the method of reporting your annuity on your tax return. If you determine that you must use the three-year rule, your entire annuity, including the increase, is fully taxable after you have received payments equaling your cost. If when you received your first annuity payment you determined that you may not use the three-year rule, a later increase in your monthly rate will not enable you to use it. A future increase in a Civil Service pension to the retiree or his survivor is not treated as annuity income but is reported in full as miscellaneous income and is not reduced by the exclusion ratio. However, an increase effective on or before a survivor's Civil Service annuity commences must be taken into account in computing the expected return or in determining the aggregate amount receivable under the annuity.

If you retired during the past year and filed your application for retirement late or are entitled to accrued payments because your application was processed late, you may receive a lump-sum payment representing the unpaid accrued monthly installments for the period before your regular monthly payments begin. If the lump sum is less than your cost of the annuity, you determine whether the three-year rule applies as explained above. Disregarding the lump sum, multiply the monthly rate of your annuity by 36; if that amount plus the lump sum equals or exceeds your cost, you must use the three-year rule. In determining your tax for the year under the three-year rule, the lump sum is treated as a tax-free recovery of part of your cost. If the lump sum exceeds your cost of the annuity, the excess is fully taxable. Also, all the regular monthly annuity payments you receive thereafter are fully taxable.

A lump-sum payment for accrued annual leave received upon retirement is not part of your annuity. It is treated as a salary payment and is taxable as ordinary income.

If you made voluntary contributions to the retirement fund, you report the portion of your annuity attributable to the voluntary contributions as a separate annuity taxable under the six-step method.

If you made voluntary contributions, an information return which you receive each year will state the portion of your monthly payments attributable to your voluntary contributions.

How beneficiaries report annuity payments

A pension annuity paid to you as the beneficiary may qualify for a death benefit exclusion, up to $5,000. The amount of the exclusion is added to the cost of the annuity in calculating the investment in the contract as of the annuity starting date. Thus if the decedent's contribution plus the death benefit exclusion will be recovered within three years of the annuity starting date, you report the annuity payments under the three-year rule.

EXAMPLE—

An employee contributed $9,000 to his annuity. When he died, his widow was entitled to $3,000 a year and his two children to $1,000 a year each. In the first three years they will receive a total of $15,000. Of this amount, $14,000 is considered a tax-free recovery of the employee's cost (cost of $9,000 plus $5,000 death benefit). In the first two years the widow and the children exclude the full amount of their pension benefits ($10,000). In the third year the remaining $4,000 to be received tax free is allocated according to the ratio of benefits received by each person; the widow receives $2,400 tax free (60% of the remaining $4,000) and each child receives $800 tax free (20% of $4,000).

The $5,000 exclusion may not be added to the investment if the deceased had received any payment under a joint and survivor contract after reaching retirement age.

If after taking the $5,000 exclusion into account in computing the investment in the contract the three-year rule is not applicable (because the contract investment exceeds the return of the first three years), the beneficiary follows the six-step method to compute taxable income. If the annuity is payable over the lifetime of the beneficiary, actuarial tables are used to determine the expected return on the contract. Ask the company paying the annuity to give you these amounts. The maximum amount of the death benefit exclusion is fixed at $5,000, without regard to the number of beneficiaries or the number of employers funding pension payments.

Military personnel allowed tax exclusion on annuity election

If, when you retire from the military, you elect to receive reduced retirement pay to provide an annuity for your spouse or certain child beneficiaries, you do not report that part of your retirement pay used to fund the annuity.

EXAMPLE—

You are eligible to receive retirement pay of $500 a month. You elect a joint and survivor annuity paying you $400 a month and $200 to your spouse on your death. You report $400 a month for tax purposes during your lifetime, rather than the $500. On your death, your spouse generally will report the full $200 a month received as income.

If you received retirement pay before 1966 and elected reduced benefits, you reported more retirement pay than you actually received. In this case, amounts attributed to the reduction in retirement pay reported in prior years offset retirement pay received in 1966 and later years.

If you elected to receive veteran's benefits instead of some or all of your retirement pay, you may have been required to deposit with the U.S. Treasury an amount equal to the reduction for the annuity. If so, you do not report retirement pay until it equals the amount deposited.

If all the retired person's consideration for the contract (previously taxed reductions) has not been offset against retirement income at the time of death, the beneficiary is entitled to a tax break. The beneficiary excludes all payments under the contract until the exclusions equal the remaining consideration for the contract not previously excluded by the deceased. As soon as this amount is excluded, the beneficiary reports all later payments as income.

The $5,000 death benefit exclusion is treated as a cost investment to be added to the spouse's annuity contract if the serviceman retired because of disability and died before reaching retirement age.

Are your retirement benefits protected from the claims of creditors and ex-spouses?

Retirement benefits, whether accrued in a company plan or saved through your IRA, make up a significant source of funds. If you are experiencing financial difficulty or if you are in the process of negotiating a divorce settlement, you may face the question of whether this source can be tapped. The answer is not clear-cut.

All qualified plans are required to contain an "anti-alienation provision" which prohibits a participant from assigning or alienating plan benefits. The reason for such a provision is to ensure that the benefits are generally not subject to attachment, garnishment, levy, execution, or other legal or equitable process. There are some exceptions.

Benefits are not shielded from enforcement of a federal tax levy or collection by the federal government on a judgment for an unpaid tax assessment.

Federal law does not prevent a creditor from attaching a regular IRA account. Recently, a New York court held that a judgment creditor can attach an IRA held by a bank-trustee. Although the IRA cannot be assigned by the owner, it can be attached by the creditor. While New York law exempts from satisfaction-of-judgment procedures the assets of a trust set up by one person for the benefit of another, the exemption does not apply to an IRA since the trust grantor and beneficiary are the same person. When an IRA account is taken by a creditor, the IRA owner must report the distribution as income. Further, if the owner is not age 59½ or over or disabled, he or she is subject to a 10% penalty for a premature withdrawal.

An IRA bond by its terms may be exempt from attachment, at least until the owner is age 59½. Similarly, an IRA annuity may be exempt since the policy, by its terms, is nontransferable.

The Bankruptcy Act of 1978 provides that, under federal law, an employee's rights under a qualified pension or profit-sharing plan are exempt from the bankruptcy estate to the extent reasonably necessary to provide for the support of the bankrupt or his dependents. One bankruptcy court refused to grant an exemption for the Keogh contributions of a debtor who was under age 59½ and not currently receiving any benefits from the plan. Its reason: the debtor had merely a future right to benefits. An appeals court agreed. The law is designed to support the bankrupt and his family, not to preserve a future asset. The exemption is purely a statutory one. Arguments of fairness and equity have no sway for purposes of the exemption. Thus there is no absolute exemption under federal law. Moreover, states have their own bankruptcy rules which may apply. A bankruptcy court in Wisconsin has held that Keogh plan contributions were not exempt from the bankrupt's estate under federal law. Similarly, a bankruptcy court in Tennessee held that contributions to a defined-contribution Keogh plan were not exempt under either Tennessee or federal law.

Marital actions. The law generally allows a spouse or former spouse to obtain rights to an employee's benefits under a pension, profit-sharing, or stock bonus plan where support or alimony obligations are in arrears. A "qualified domestic relations order" must be obtained from a state court. To qualify, the "domestic relations order" must give a spouse, former spouse, child or other dependent of the employee a right to the benefits because of the employee's obligation to pay alimony, marital property rights, or child support. The court order may not require the plan to provide any type of benefit not otherwise allowed or require increased benefits. The order may require payments for a spouse or child as of the earliest retirement age under the plan, even though the employee is still working.

Other tests and special rules apply to qualified domestic relations orders. The advice of an experienced tax practitioner is required to conform to the rules.

Withholding tax on pension benefits

Pension benefits and IRA distributions are automatically subject to withholding. For many recipients, withholding avoids the need to pay estimated tax. However, if you choose, you may elect to avoid withholding.

Withholding on annuities and other periodic payments exceeding $5,400 annually is based on the wage withholding

120 IRA, KEOGH, AND OTHER RETIREMENT PLANS

tables. No tax is withheld on payments of $450 a month or less.

For lump-sum payments, a special withholding table takes into account the ten-year averaging method. The table applies if the distribution consists of an entire plan balance and is paid within one calendar year, even if other tests for ten-year averaging have not been met.

Chapter 8
RETIREMENT BENEFIT OPTIONS AND ROLLOVERS

BEFORE you reach retirement age, you should consider how and when you will take your retirement benefits. Project how much you will be entitled to receive from your plan upon retirement. If you are covered by a company plan, remember that your benefits must be "vested" in order for you to receive them. Will you take distributions in a lump sum or on an annuity basis? Your choice of payment method will affect your tax. For example, lump-sum distributions receive more favorable tax treatment than annuities.

Are your employee benefits vested?

If you are covered by a company plan, you are not assured of a payout upon retirement unless you have vested benefits. If you retire or leave the company before the number of years specified in the company's vesting schedule, you will not receive all the benefits which have accrued on your behalf.

As an employee, your benefits from your own contributions are always 100% vested. The law provides minimum vesting requirements for benefits from employer contributions. Your company must adopt a vesting schedule which is at least as beneficial as *one* of the following:

1. Full vesting after ten years. When you have completed ten years of service, your benefits from employer contributions are 100% vested. If you leave the company before completing ten years of service, you are not entitled to any benefits.

2. Gradual vesting. After five years of service, 25% of your accrued benefits from employer contributions become nonforfeitable. For each of the next five years vested benefits increase by 5%, so that after ten years your benefits are 50% vested. For each of the next five years vesting increases by 10%, so that after 15 years your benefits are 100% vested.

3. Rule of 45 vesting. Your benefits are 50% vested when your age plus years of service total at least 45, or after ten years of service, whichever occurs first. Once your benefits are 50% vested, 10% is vested for each additional year of service.

4. Class-year plans. Your company may vest each year's contribution separately. In such plans your benefits from employer contributions must be 100% vested no later than the end of the fifth plan year after the year of the contribution.

5. Special vesting for top-heavy plans. If you are covered by a plan that is determined to be top heavy, special vesting rules apply. These rules are discussed in Chapter 4.

Keep in mind that these are minimum vesting requirements. Your company may allow more rapid vesting. Ask the administrator of your company plan to give you a copy of the plan description which includes the vesting schedule.

Generally, you will be credited with a year of service if you have worked 1,000 hours in a consecutive 12-month period. The company does not have to include years of service before age 18 unless it uses the rule of 45 to determine vesting. If, before you had any vested benefits, you had a "break in service" (i.e., you worked no more than 500 hours within a 12-month period), your company does not have to count your employment before the break if it is less than the period of the break itself.

In some cases a plan may have different years of service requirements: one for figuring accrued benefits and another for vesting purposes. Your plan administrator can tell you if your accrued and vested benefits differ.

When to take retirement benefits

When you should take retirement benefits is a decision governed in part by the terms of your plan and in part by personal

RETIREMENT BENEFIT OPTIONS AND ROLLOVERS

wishes and needs. Here are the earliest and latest dates you may receive benefits without tax penalty or loss of tax advantages.

For years starting after 1984, common rules apply to distributions made to employees and self-employed persons.

You may receive distributions before the age of 59½ without penalty provided you did not have an equity interest of more than 5% while a member of the plan. A 10% penalty applies to the extent the taxable portion of the distribution is allocated to contributions made while you held an interest of 5% or more. The penalty does not apply to distributions received because of death or disability.

Employees must start to receive distributions by April 1 of the year following the *later* of the calendar year they reach age 70½ or the calendar year of retirement. However, a person who has an interest of more than 5% during the plan year ending in the calendar year in which he or she reaches age 70½ must start to receive distributions by the following April 1, whether or not retired.

A more than 5% owner who is age 70½ before the start of the first plan year beginning after 1984 must start to receive distributions by April 1, 1986.

Important: The above rules on earliest and latest distribution dates would be toughened by tax law proposals.

Pre-1984 designations. Individuals who made a special election before 1984 to receive distributions under pre-1984 rules are not subject to the age 70½ rule or the beneficiary distribution rules discussed below.

Distribution methods. For plan years beginning after 1984, the following distribution methods apply to employees and self-employed individuals. Payments may be spread over life expectancy or over the lives or life expectancies of the participant and any designated beneficiary. Life expectancy may be recalculated annually for an employee and his or her spouse.

If a participant dies before receiving his entire interest, the balance must be distributed to beneficiaries at least as rapidly as under the method the participant was using. If he dies before receiving any benefits, his interest must generally be distributed within five years after death with these exceptions. If a surviving spouse is the beneficiary, and a joint and survivor annuity was elected, distributions follow that method. Otherwise, distributions do not have to start until the date on which the deceased would have reached age 70½; starting on that date, the surviving spouse must receive distributions over his or her life or life expectancy. If someone other than a surviving spouse is beneficiary, distributions may be spread over the beneficiary's life or life expectancy, provided that distributions begin no later than one year after the deceased's death. The IRS may extend the one-year limit if circumstances warrant a delay.

Governmental plans and collective-bargaining plans. The above distribution rules do not apply to government retirement plans until plan years starting after 1986. For collectively bargained plans ratified on or before July 18, 1984, the above rules generally do not apply until the earlier of January 1, 1988, or the date on which the bargaining agreement terminates (without regard to extensions after July 18, 1984).

How to take retirement benefits

Whether you will receive benefits monthly, quarterly, or in a lump sum may be determined by your retirement plan. Some qualified plans will only pay benefits as an annuity. If you are married, your plan must provide by law for benefits in the form of a qualified joint and survivor annuity, although with your spouse's written consent, you may elect a different form of benefit such as a lump sum. See Chapter 4 for details. If you are given the option of how to take benefits, consider not only your personal and financial needs but the tax consequences of your choice. Lump-sum distributions receive favorable tax treatment.

When you receive a lump-sum distribution from a qualified plan, you face a choice: Should you opt to have the use of your money but pay tax now, or defer tax but do without the use of the money? Personal considerations may require that you take the money now and therefore pay tax now. However, if personal considerations do not dictate your decision, tax effects should be considered.

If you must pay tax now, you might qualify for averaging. New law proposals on averaging are discussed at the end of this book.

Is a rollover advisable when you retire?

THE transfer of a lump-sum distribution to a qualified pension plan or IRA is called a rollover. A rollover allows you to defer tax on lump-sum distributions. A qualifying partial distribution may be rolled over to an IRA.

The decision to make a rollover involves an evaluation of present and future needs as well as the tax consequences of the rollover.

When you receive a qualified lump-sum distribution, you have only 60 days to decide whether to postpone tax by making a rollover to an IRA or pay tax now using the favorable ten-year averaging method. After 60 days, a rollover may not be made. If you need the funds immediately, take the distribution and pay the tax. Similarly, if you think you may have to withdraw the entire account in a few years, a rollover may be unwise because a distribution of the rolled-over account will be immediately taxed as ordinary income; special averaging is not allowed for an IRA distribution. If you qualify for special averaging but do not plan to use the funds until retirement, estimate whether you will build a larger retirement fund by rolling over the distribution and letting earnings accumulate tax free, or by using special averaging and investing the funds to give you the greatest after-tax return. This is not an easy projection. You must consider the number of years to retirement, your expected tax bracket at retirement, and the estimated yield you can earn on your funds. Generally speaking, a younger person who is not planning to retire for many years will probably obtain a greater after-tax return by making a rollover and investing at peak rates, and then taking withdrawals over his life expectancy at retirement. However, a rollover to an IRA bars you from withdrawing funds without a penalty before age 59½, unless you are disabled.

Rules for making a tax-free rollover into an IRA or a qualified plan

A lump-sum distribution from a qualified plan is not taxable if within 60 days it is transferred in whole or in part to a qualified plan of your new employer or to an IRA which you set up on your own behalf.

To make a tax-free rollover from a qualified plan to an IRA or another qualified plan, your lump-sum distribution must meet these tests:

1. The distribution must be all that is due you under the plan. That is, if your employer's plan uses more than one trust, you must receive a distribution of all that is due you from each trust.
2. The payment or payments must be made within one of your taxable years.
3. The distribution must be made because you are separated from service, reach age 59½, or the plan has been terminated,

If any part of a distribution is attributable to contributions made while you were a more than 5% owner in a top-heavy plan, you may make a rollover only to an IRA and not to another qualified plan.

You do not have to make a rollover of your entire account; you may roll over part of the distribution and keep part of it. The rolled-over portion is tax free. The amount not rolled over is currently taxable. However, because you have rolled over a portion of the total funds, you may not use special ten-year averaging or capital gain treatment for the taxable amount even though you could have used these methods if you had not made a rollover.

You may make a rollover even though you do not qualify for ten-year averaging because you were not a plan participant for five years before retirement.

You may make a rollover to an IRA even though you are age 70½ provided you begin to take minimum distributions.

A surviving spouse may roll over to an IRA a lump-sum distribution paid on the death of a spouse or upon termination of a qualified retirement plan. Such a rollover may not include benefits attributable to the deceased's nondeductible contributions to the plan. The distribution may not be rolled over to a qualified plan of the surviving spouse's current employer.

If you receive property, such as your employer's stock, as

part of your distribution, you must roll over the same property or sell it and roll over the sales proceeds as discussed later in this chapter.

The amount you roll over may not include your nondeductible contributions to the qualified plan. However, if you make deductible voluntary contributions to your employer's plan, you must include your contributions in a tax-free rollover.

You may not claim a deduction for your rollover contribution to an IRA even if you did not use up your IRA contribution limit for the year.

An IRA account may be used as a conduit between two company plans. The funds in the IRA account may be transferred to another qualified plan of a company for which you work, provided the plan of your new employer accepts rollovers. The IRA account must consist of only the assets (or proceeds from the sale of such assets) previously distributed from the first qualified plan and income earned on the account. You may not contribute to the account set up as a conduit. If you are not immediately employed or are employed by a company not having a qualified plan, you may set up another IRA account to which you may make annual contributions. In such a case you will have two accounts: one consisting of the assets (or proceeds from the sale of such assets) of the plan of your prior employer and the other of your own contributions.

EXAMPLE—

You leave your employer and receive a lump-sum distribution of $5,000 from his qualified plan to which you did not contribute. You place the amount in an IRA account. Four years later you start work for another company that has a qualified plan. The new plan permits you to transfer the assets of the IRA to the plan. You must make the transfer within 60 days after closing the IRA account.

When the distribution is substantial, you may wish to divide it and put portions into different investments. Diversification is permissible. There is no limit on the number of rollover accounts you may have. A lump-sum distribution may be rolled over to several IRAs or retirement annuities.

Rollover of annuities for employees of tax-exempt groups and schools. If you participate in a tax-sheltered annuity program, you may roll over a lump-sum distribution to an IRA.

Changing a rollover election

Suppose you make a rollover but later decide that you would have been better off paying tax currently using ten-year averaging. Can you undo your rollover election? In a 1979 private letter ruling, the IRS allowed a retired person to change to ten-year averaging after making a rollover. However, in 1985 private letter rulings, the IRS reversed itself and refused to allow ten-year averaging after making an IRA rollover. Once a rollover is made, the right to use ten-year averaging is lost. Any withdrawals from the rollover account are 100% taxable as IRA distributions.

Rollover of proceeds from sale of property received in lump-sum distribution

A lump-sum distribution from a qualified plan may include property, such as stock. If you plan to roll over the distribution, you may find that a bank may not want to take the property. If you sell the property for this or another reason, you may roll over the sale proceeds to an IRA as long as the sale and rollover take place within 60 days of the receipt of the distribution. If you roll over all the proceeds, no tax is incurred on any gain realized on the sale. Similarly, if you realize a loss it is not deductible. The proceeds are treated as part of the distribution. If you make a partial rollover, you incur tax on the retained proceeds, and in reporting the taxable amount you allocate between ordinary income and capital gain elements according to the following special formulas.

If you receive cash and property in your distribution and you sell the property but make a partial rollover, you must designate the amount of cash to be treated as part of the rollover. The designation must be made by the time for filing your return (plus any extensions) and is irrevocable. If you do not make a timely designation, the allocation between cash and proceeds is made on a ratable basis.

RETIREMENT BENEFIT OPTIONS AND ROLLOVERS

The distribution to the extent of your contributions to the plan may not be rolled over to an IRA. See Treasury regulations for the effect of employee contributions on an allocation.

Rollovers of IRAs

You may transfer assets tax free from one IRA to another. Such transfers are treated as a distribution of the assets from your old plan to you. To avoid tax on the transfer, these tests must be met: (1) You must transfer the amount you receive from your old plan to the new plan within 60 days. (2) A tax-free rollover may occur only once within a one-year period. If you make another rollover within the same one-year period, you are taxed on the plan assets as they are distributed to you.

As long as funds are not distributed to you, a transfer or reinvestment is not considered a rollover. Thus if your CD matures and you direct the bank to renew the CD for another term, you have not made a rollover. Similarly, a transfer of funds from one bank to another may not constitute a rollover subject to the one-year restriction.

EXAMPLE—

Smith sets up an IRA at Bank A. He later instructs Bank A to transfer the funds to Bank B. The transfer from Bank A to Bank B is not subject to the one-year restriction on rollovers because there was no payment or distribution of the funds to Smith.

According to proposed Treasury regulations, the one-year rule applies to each IRA you have. For example, you have an IRA at your local bank as well as an IRA annuity with your insurance company. In 1986 you make a tax-free rollover of your annuity to a mutual fund IRA. You may also roll over your bank IRA in 1986.

You have not made a tax-free rollover if you take a distribution from your IRA and use it to buy an endowment policy. The distribution is included in your income and is subject to tax.

Partial rollover. You need not make a complete rollover of the distribution to ensure tax-free treatment. You may make a partial rollover. The part rolled over is not taxed; the part of the distribution you retain is taxable.

Rollovers of inherited IRAs. A surviving spouse may roll over the IRA account of a deceased spouse. Nonspouse beneficiaries must start taking distributions.

Tax-free transfer of an IRA because of divorce

A spouse may transfer his IRA account or individual retirement annuity tax free to his former spouse. As long as the transfer is made under a valid divorce decree or written agreement incident to the divorce, there are no tax consequences to either party, provided the transferred account or annuity is maintained in the name of the spouse who receives it.

Chapter 9
SOCIAL SECURITY

SOCIAL Security is a government program designed to provide workers and their dependents with retirement funds and other benefits.

The Social Security program provides four types of benefits:

1. Retirement benefits for workers and for spouses and dependent children of retirees. These benefits currently begin at age 65, or at a reduced level at age 62.

2. Survivor's benefits for the spouse, minor children, and dependent elderly parents of a worker who dies.

3. Disability benefits for a worker who is unable to work for an extended period. Benefits are also paid to the spouse and children of a disabled worker.

4. Medical insurance (Medicare) beginning at age 65 and for disabled workers who have been receiving disability payments for at least 24 months.

Qualifying for benefits

You must work for a required period of time in covered employment to obtain insured status. The required time depends on your age or the date of your retirement, death, or disability. There are two types of coverage, currently insured status and fully insured status. If you have worked for at least ten years in covered employment, you are fully insured, regardless of your age. If you have not, you may still qualify under one of several tests which give insured status even if you have less than ten years in covered employment.

Currently insured status. This protection is designed to help families of those who die without having enough coverage to qualify for retirement benefits.

If you are currently insured at the time you die, survivor benefits are payable to:

Your unmarried children (or dependent grandchildren whose parents are dead or disabled) if under 18 or disabled, regardless of their ages.

Your spouse (or divorced spouse), if caring for your child under 18.

Also payable under the currently insured status are lump-sum death benefits to a spouse or eligible child.

Fully insured status. If you have fully insured status, you and your family may receive retirement and disability benefits, and your family also receives protection in case of your death. Retirement benefits are payable to the following:

The insured worker, age 62 or over.
Spouse or divorced spouse, age 62 or over.
Spouse, any age, if caring for child under age 18.
Children or grandchildren (if qualified as above).

In addition, survivor's benefits are paid as under the *currently insured* section, and *fully insured status* may also provide survivor benefits to:

Widow, widower, or divorced spouse, age 60 or over; earlier if disabled.
Dependent parent, age 62 or over.

Working wives should note that they have their own earnings record and can collect benefits on their own. They need not wait until their husbands retire to collect benefits. Working spouses receive the higher of the worker's benefit or the spousal benefit, but not both.

A divorced spouse may collect on the account of his or her former retired spouse (the insured worker) if the marriage lasted ten years or longer before ending in divorce. If the insured worker remarries, the divorce spouse may still collect on his or her account, even if the insured's new spouse is also collecting. But if the nonworking divorced spouse remarries, he or she may not collect on the former spouse's account. The remarried spouse can collect only on the account of the new spouse. However, if the second marriage ends in divorce after ten years, he or she may collect on the account of either former spouse if both former spouses were insured. If the second marriage ends in divorce in less than ten years, he or she may collect only on the account of the first spouse. But if the insured spouse of the second marriage dies after one year, the uninsured spouse may collect on the account of the deceased.

EXAMPLES—

1. Paul and Joan Brown divorce after 12 years of marriage. Joan does not work. Paul remarries but Joan does not. When Paul retires, both Joan and Paul's second wife may collect on his account.

2. Same as above but following the divorce from Paul, Joan marries Sam. She may collect only on Sam's account. If the second marriage ends in divorce after ten years, she may collect on either Paul's or Sam's account. If the second marriage had not lasted ten years, Joan would have been able to collect only on Paul's account.

A divorced person who takes care of a former spouse's children is eligible for benefits when the former spouse dies or retires, even if the marriage did not last ten years. Children of a divorced couple are eligible for dependents' or survivors' benefits on the record of either parent. Their benefits are not affected by the custody or support arrangements of their divorced parents.

Benefits to a widow or widower usually end if he or she remarries. However, this rule does not apply if the widow or widower is age 60 or older when the second marriage takes place. An individual may receive a benefit on the account of the new spouse if it would be larger than the widow's or widower's benefit.

There is a ceiling on the amount of benefits that may be paid on one worker's account. This limit is calculated using a formula based on the worker's earnings.

Keep a record of credits. You should keep a record of your earnings and payments of Social Security taxes (FICA). The Social Security Administration has been criticized for not keeping up with workers' earnings records. Do not risk a problem by ignoring your record. At least once every three years, you should mail Form SSA-7004, Request for Statement of Earnings, to the Social Security Administration, Wilkes-Barre Data Operations Center, P.O. Box 20, Wilkes-Barre, PA. 18703. This form is available at your local Social Security office and at the headquarters in Baltimore. You will receive a response in about six weeks. Compare it with your records.

Social Security forms state that if you wait more than three years, three months, and 15 days after an error is discovered to request a correction, a change may not be possible. The agency waived the deadline in 1981 since it had fallen behind in its recordkeeping, but you should still try to correct any errors immediately.

Applying for Social Security retirement benefits

You should make your application to collect benefits at the local Social Security office three months before your 62nd or 65th birthday, depending on the year you plan to retire. This allows enough time for your claim to be processed and to locate all necessary information.

You cannot collect Social Security benefits without applying for them. The government is not obligated to remind you of your rights or benefits. You must contact your local Social Security office for information and to begin the collection process. It is advisable to call before going to the office so you will know which personal papers, such as proof of your age, you must bring with you.

Payment of benefits

Social Security checks are mailed to reach a beneficiary on the third of the month following the benefit month. That is, you receive your January check on February 3. When a husband and wife are both receiving benefits, they usually receive one check for the total amount. If you prefer, you may request separate checks. For your convenience and safety, you may have your check deposited directly in your account at a bank or thrift institution by filling out Standard Form 1199, Authorization for Deposit of Social Security Payments, available at your financial institution.

Estimating retirement benefits

How much you receive from Social Security at retirement depends on your earnings history. For years there was a guaranteed minimum benefit, but legislation in 1981 ended this minimum for persons retiring in 1982 and later years.

The amount of your benefit may be adjusted each year to account for increases in the cost of living. There have been increases every year since 1976 when this provision went into effect.

If you are age 55 or older, your local Social Security office can provide an estimate of your retirement benefits. You may request a pamphlet entitled "Estimating Your Social Security Retirement Check" at a local office. However, determining your own monthly benefit is difficult because the formula provided is very complicated.

Below is a projection of benefits for individuals retiring at ages 62 and 65 in upcoming years. These are only estimates; actual benefits will depend on a worker's earnings and the cost of living.

AVERAGE ANNUAL BENEFITS

Retirement year	Retired worker age 62	Retired worker age 65
1985	$5,476	$6,666
1986	5,676	7,156
1987	5,983	7,612
1988	6,319	7,959
1989	6,684	8,175
1990	7,040	8,560
1995	9,236	11,149
2000	12,068	14,605

Social Security and retirement planning

For many, Social Security is a necessary mainstay of their retirement income. However, Social Security benefits can only cover some basic needs, and thus should not be the only source of funds in your retirement plans. A substantial savings account, a retirement account, income from investments, and in some cases, work after retirement should supplement Social Security benefits.

Should you retire early? Your decision must take into account your overall financial picture, as well as your personal goals and work opportunities. We consider here only the effect of your decision on Social Security benefits. If you choose to retire early, you may do so and begin to receive benefits at age 62 (generally in the month following your birthday). However, the amount of your monthly benefits is permanently reduced. The reduction is figured by a formula based on the number of months before age 65 that you retire. If you retire at the earliest age, 62, your monthly benefit is reduced by about 20%. If you live until age 77, retiring at age 62 means that you will receive more total benefits from the system than if you delay retirement until 65. Age 77 is the break-even point at which it makes no overall difference whether you opted for early retirement. Beyond age 77, you receive more benefits if you wait until age 65 to retire.

Should you delay retirement? If you do not retire at age 65, you increase the retirement benefit you will receive when you retire. For those born in 1916 or earlier, the increase is 1% per year for each year of delayed retirement; for those born in 1917 or later, the increase is 3% a year. No additional credit accrues in the month you reach 70 and thereafter. Starting in 1990, workers who delay retirement past age 65 will receive larger benefits. The 3% figure will increase in stages until the additional benefit for delayed retirement reaches 8% in 2009.

Your Social Security benefits may be reduced if you earn

wages or self-employment income. If you are under 70, you are allowed to receive a flat amount of earned income before benefits are reduced. After earnings exceed the base amount, benefits are reduced $1 for every $2 of earnings. When you reach age 70, you may earn any amount of earned income without losing Social Security benefits. The base amount for reducing benefits is modified periodically for changes in the cost of living index. In 1986, retirees between the ages of 65 and 69 may earn up to $7,800 without losing benefits. Once earnings exceed $7,800, benefits are reduced $1 for every $2 of earnings. Starting in 1990, benefits will be reduced $1 for every $3 of earnings over the base amount.

As long as you continue to work, you pay Social Security taxes on your earnings, regardless of your age.

How Social Security benefits are taxed

Up to 50% of your benefits may be taxed if your income exceeds a base amount. Whether your benefits are taxable depends on the amount of your benefits and your other income. For purposes of figuring taxable benefits, tax-exempt interest is counted as income. At the time this book went to press, Congress was considering a measure to disregard tax-exempt interest from the Social Security computation.

There are two steps in figuring the taxation of Social Security benefits: (1) Figuring whether your income exceeds a base amount for your filing status. (2) Figuring the amount of benefits subject to tax.

Step 1. Start with adjusted gross income. Add to it 50% of your Social Security benefits, tax-exempt interest, excluded foreign earned income, and the marriage penalty deduction. Part of your benefits are taxable if your adjusted gross income increased by step (1) exceeds $25,000 and you are single or $32,000 and you are married filing jointly.

EXAMPLES—

1. In 1986, you are married and have dividend and interest income of $28,000 and tax-exempt interest of $2,000. Your Social Security benefits are $4,000 and you file a joint return.

IRA, KEOGH, AND OTHER RETIREMENT PLANS

Adjusted gross income		$28,000
Plus: Tax-exempt interest	$2,000	
50% of benefits	2,000	4,000
		32,000
Less: Base amount		32,000
		0

Your benefits are not taxable.

2. Same as above except your Social Security benefits are $8,000.

Adjusted gross income		$28,000
Plus: Tax-exempt interest	$2,000	
50% of benefits	4,000	6,000
		$34,000
Less: Base amount		32,000
Excess		$ 2,000

Part of your benefits are subject to tax under the rules of Step 2.

Step 2. The amount of benefits subject to tax is 50% of the excess over the base amount or 50% of benefits, whichever is less.

EXAMPLE—

In example 2 above, $1,000 of benefits are subject to tax because 50% of the excess over the base amount (50% of $2,000) is less than 50% of benefits (50% of $8,000).

If you are married and file a separate return, one half of your benefits is automatically subject to tax. If you live apart from your spouse at all times during the year and file separately, the $25,000 base for singles applies.

In the chart on page 146, the column in the center lists how much income you may receive before benefits become taxable. The last column lists the levels at which 50% of benefits become taxable.

Medicare coverage

When you apply for Social Security benefits at age 65, your enrollment in Part A Medicare, covering hospitalization, is automatic. At the same time, you may enroll in Part B, covering medical-surgical expenses. For this protection, you pay a monthly premium, which is usually deducted from monthly Social Security payments. Even if you are not retired, you become eligible for Medicare at age 65 and should take advantage of it, even if you also have medical coverage through your employer's plan. Postponing enrollment until retirement may result in a delay in Medicare coverage for more than a year. You may enroll in Medicare B only in January, February, or March; coverage begins the following July.

A worker's spouse is eligible for Medicare when he or she reaches age 65.

If you do not choose to enroll in Part B when you turn 65, you may enroll later, but your premium will be 10% higher for each year you delay enrollment. Also, if you enroll in Medicare Part B and then drop out, you are subject to a higher premium if you choose to enroll again later. You pay this higher premium the rest of your life.

There is no premium for Part A, Hospital Insurance, if you meet Social Security work requirements. If you are not eligible for benefits, you may still obtain Part A coverage by paying a monthly premium.

Part B, Supplementary Medical Insurance, partially covers the services of physicians and surgeons and certain medical and health services. It currently pays 80% of "reasonable charges." The patient is liable for an annual deductible, the remaining 20% of costs, and any amounts considered above "reasonable charges." For Part B, a doctor can choose whether to accept the assignment, that is, if he or she will accept Medicare's reasonable charges as his or her fee. If the doctor agrees, Medicare pays 80%, you pay 20%, and the bill is considered paid in full. If your doctor does not accept the assignment, Medicare still pays 80% according to its schedule of reasonable fees, but you must pay the difference between Medicare's payment and your doctor's actual charge.

Part B also pays for certain durable medical equipment, such as crutches or a hospital bed. It does not pay for equipment inappropriate to the home and items that are considered personal conveniences. Check with your local Medicare office about whether specific items would be covered. Also, find out whether it would be more practical to rent rather than buy such equipment.

IRA, KEOGH, AND OTHER RETIREMENT PLANS
EFFECT OF OTHER INCOME ON SOCIAL SECURITY

Single

Monthly Social Security benefits	No benefits taxed unless other income exceeds—	50% of benefits taxed if other income is at least—
$ 300	$23,200	$26,800
350	22,900	27,100
400	22,600	27,400
450	22,300	27,700
500	22,000	28,000
550	21,700	28,300
600	21,400	28,600
650	21,100	28,900
700	20,800	29,200
750	20,500	29,500
800	20,200	29,800
850	19,900	30,100
900	19,600	30,400
950	19,300	30,700
1,000	19,000	31,000

Married filing jointly

Monthly Social Security benefits	No benefits taxed unless other income exceeds—	50% of benefits taxed if other income is at least—
$ 700	$27,800	$36,200
750	27,500	36,500
800	27,200	36,800
850	26,900	37,100
900	26,600	37,400
950	26,300	37,700
1,000	26,000	38,000
1,050	25,700	38,300
1,100	25,400	38,600
1,150	25,100	38,900
1,200	24,800	39,200
1,250	24,500	39,500
1,300	24,200	39,800
1,350	23,900	40,100
1,400	23,600	40,400

Filing claims

For Part A the provider of services, for example, the hospital, sends the claims to Medicare which pays the hospital directly. You only have to sign the claim form to verify that you received the stated services.

For Part B, if your doctor accepts the assignment, he or she files the claim and is paid directly by Medicare. If your doctor does not accept the assignment, you must file Form 1490S to receive reimbursement from Medicare. To make sure your claims are processed, file claims as soon as possible. Medicare allows you at least 15 months to file a claim, depending on the month your claim is incurred. For example, if your claim is for services received between October 1, 1985 and September 30, 1986, you have until December 31, 1987 to file your claim.

What Medicare does not cover

Below are some major items which Medicare will not pay for:

1. Custodial care that does not require the services of trained medical personnel. This includes care in a residential nursing home and help in preparing meals or getting around at home.
2. Preventive health care, such as annual checkups.
3. Glasses, contact lenses, and hearing aids and examinations to determine whether you need any of these items.
4. Cosmetic surgery.
5. Items considered personal comfort items rather than medical necessities, for example, a telephone in your hospital room.
6. The first three pints of blood needed during a hospital stay.
7. Most dental care.
8. Most foot care.
9. Injections that can be self-administered, such as insulin.
10. Generally, health care outside the United States.

Medicare and additional health insurance

Retirees spend substantially more on health care than younger workers. When planning for your future expenses, health insurance is a necessity for which you must provide. While Medicare covers some charges, as explained in the prior pages, rising costs in the Medicare program which must be borne by the patient weigh heavily on the retiree with diminished income. If your company has no retiree health insurance coverage to supplement Medicare, you must buy individual policies to help cover the gaps in both Part A and B. The federal government certifies those so-called medigap policies that meet federal standards. Be sure to obtain approved coverage; many retirees have been victimized in the past by inadequate, unnecessary, and high-priced policies. You can obtain a free booklet, "Guide to Health Insurance for People With Medicare," by writing to the Department of Health and Human Services, Health Care Financing Administration, Baltimore, Maryland 21207.

When you shop for a policy, find out first whether your employer provides a health insurance plan to retired workers or whether the policy you had through your job may be converted to an individual policy upon retirement. Blue Cross/Blue Shield policies are often convertible. Continuing the same policy has advantages: there is no lapse in coverage and you do not have to worry about "preexisting" conditions.

Many medigap policies are designed to coordinate benefits with your Medicare coverage. However, read such policies carefully; some costs will still not be covered. For example, most supplementary policies, like Medicare, do not pay for regular checkups. Other policies pay you cash but do not pay particular bills.

Chapter 10
ESTATE TAX ON RETIREMENT BENEFITS

RETIREMENT benefits may make up a sizable portion of your estate. Bank advertisements promise million-dollar funds for young workers who contribute the maximum amount annually to an IRA until retirement. Benefits from qualified pension or profit-sharing plans or Keogh plans will boost the amount. Benefits of key employees in closely-held corporations may exceed $1 million from company plans alone. While it is impossible to figure the exact amount of your retirement benefits in 20 or 30 years, you should be able to project how much they would be if you died today, or in five years or ten years. If you are covered by a company plan, ask your plan administrator for some projections. Similarly, the trustee or custodian of your IRA can tell you your current holdings and how much they will be at the end of, say, your certificate term. Determining the size of the retirement fund will allow you to plan for its disposition and may reduce the tax liability on the distribution.

How benefits from qualified plans are taxed

Distributions from qualified retirement plans, including Keogh plans and IRAs, are not taxed when:

1. The estate (including retirement benefits) reduced by deductible expenses is less than the estate tax floor; or
2. Benefits are paid to a surviving spouse.

Further, an estate tax exclusion of up to $100,000 is allowed for annuity benefits if you were a participant in a retirement plan and in pay status (receiving benefits) as of December 31, 1984 and in addition, you irrevocably designated the form of benefits before July 18, 1984. If these conditions are satisfied, the value of an annuity, up to $100,000, received by a beneficiary other than your estate is not subject to estate tax. The $100,000 limit applies to aggregate annuities from qualified plans and IRAs.

With these rules in mind, here are some suggestions for naming recipients. You may want all or part of the benefits paid to your estate if the estate consists of substantial nonliquid assets and the benefits are needed to pay administrative costs and estate taxes.

Where little or no estate tax is estimated the decision to make benefits payable directly to beneficiaries or distributable through the estate may not be crucial unless you want to save administrative costs by having benefits pass outside the probate estate.

If retirement benefits are includable in the estate under the above rules, the new law allows payments to be spread over the life or life expectancy of the beneficiary. *See* the discussion on retirement distributions in Chapter 7.

Individual retirement plans (IRAs)

If an IRA owner dies before his entire interest has been distributed, the payment of the balance may be made to his surviving spouse or other designated beneficiary over his or her life or life expectancy, as discussed in Chapter 2.

Over the course of your working career substantial IRA benefits may accumulate. If benefits are payable to your spouse it does not matter how payment is made; while benefits will be included in the estate, they will not be taxed because of the marital deduction. However, income tax consequences may determine your spouse's choice of payment method since all IRA benefits are taxed as ordinary income when received.

Benefits paid to your estate are subject to estate tax. If the form of your beneficiary's benefits was designated before July 18, 1984 and you started to receive benefits by December 31, 1984, a $100,000 estate tax exclusion may apply. The $100,000 exclusion applies to the aggregate of all retirement benefits. The $100,000 exclusion covers any IRA benefits received in a series of substantially equal payments made for the life of the beneficiary or over a period ending at least 36 months after the decedent's death, subject to this limitation. Payments are not considered substantially equal if the amounts payable during a 12-month period exceed 40% of the total benefits payable (as determined on the date of the decedent's death). When the beneficiary is given an option to take periodic payments or payments at other intervals, benefits will be excluded only if periodic payments are elected no later than the date the estate tax return is filed. The election is made by filing an election with the IRA trustee requiring the trustee to pay out the proceeds as an annuity over at least three years or use the funds to buy an annuity contract.

If a person made excess contributions to an IRA that were not corrected prior to death, a portion of the benefits is included in the estate. The excludable portion is determined according to a special formula contained in proposed Treasury regulations.

Benefits from IRA rollover accounts are treated in the same manner as IRAs, provided that the initial rollover was from a qualifying plan, such as a retirement annuity purchased by an exempt organization.

IRAs of nonworking spouses. IRAs of nonworking spouses are treated in the same manner as regular IRAs. If benefits are payable to other than the nonworking spouse's estate, the beneficiary should ascertain whether the limited $100,000 exclusion for periodic payments is available under the rules discussed above.

How death benefits under nonqualified plans are taxed

Employers may offer plans, such as deferred-compensation plans, permanent disability benefits, and unfunded survivor's benefit plans, to pay benefits on an employee's death. Here are guidelines for determining whether benefits to which your survivors may be entitled will be taxable.

Benefits are included in the employee's estate under these circumstances:

1. The employee had the right under the contract or plan to name or change the beneficiaries, or to change the amounts payable to the beneficiaries.

2. The employee had the right to receive an annuity or other payment (alone or with another person, such as a spouse) for his or her life or for a stated number of years or for any period which does not end before death under any form of contract or agreement. "Other" payments include only post-employment benefits.

3. The employee's estate has a contingent interest in the property in excess of 5% of its value. That is, the estate could receive more than 5% of the value of the benefits. For example, an employee arranged to have a fixed death benefit paid to his wife upon his death; if she predeceased him, the benefit was to be paid to his estate. Since his estate had a contingent interest in excess of 5% of the value of the death benefit (there was the possibility that the estate would receive 100% of the benefit in the event of the wife's premature death), it was includable in his estate.

Benefits are not included under these circumstances:

1. An employee has the right to temporary salary continuation under a sickness and accident plan.

2. Benefits are paid from life insurance in which the deceased had no incidents of ownership.

Treatment of special retirement benefits

Servicemen's survivorship annuities. The value of annuities for a surviving spouse and certain child beneficiaries under the Retired Serviceman's Family Protection Plan or the Survivor's Benefit Plan is excluded from the estate except to the extent of amounts deposited by a retired serviceman pursuant to Sections 1438 or 1452(d) of Title 10 of the U.S. Code.

Mine Safety Act benefits. A survivor's annuity under Title IV of the Coal Mine Health and Safety Act of 1969 is not included in the gross estate.

Social Security Act benefits. Lump-sum death payments to a surviving spouse are excluded from the estate, as are lump-sum benefits paid to any person to the extent they are used for burial expenses. Also excluded is a monthly annuity paid to a surviving spouse age 60 or over who has not remarried.

Railroad Retirement Act benefits. Lump-sum benefits under the Railroad Retirement Act are excluded if paid to a surviving spouse or parents under age 60. Surviving spouses and parents age 60 or older are entitled to other benefits under the act which are not excludable. Similarly, residual death benefits under Section 5(f)(2) of the act are includable if a decedent may designate beneficiaries.

Civil Service retirement benefits. The U.S. Civil Service Retirement System is considered a qualified pension plan. Thus benefits are included or excluded according to the rules discussed above.

Workmen's compensation. Death benefits under state workmen's compensation laws to a dependent of an employee dying from an occupational disease are excluded from the employee's estate.

Chapter 11
GUIDE TO TAX REFORM PROPOSALS

WHEN this book went to press, Congress was considering tax proposals that would eliminate or modify several tax advantages provided by the current laws discussed in the text, such as 10-year averaging for lump-sum distributions. Generally, the proposals would take effect for tax years beginning after 1985, but in some cases more favorable transition rules may be available.

Spousal IRAs

Present law. An individual may deduct contributions to an IRA up to the lower of earned income or $2,000 each year. A married couple on a joint return may deduct up to $2,250 if one spouse has earned income of at least $2,250 and the other spouse has no earnings for the year. If both spouses have earned income, then the IRA deduction for each spouse is limited to earned income. For example, a spouse, whose only earned income for a year is $50 from jury duty, may deduct only $50.

Proposal. The total IRA deduction of a married couple could not be less than $2,250, as long as the total earned income of the couple is at least $2,250. Thus, the fact that one spouse had earnings of less than $250 would not limit the full spousal IRA deduction.

Penalty on early IRA withdrawals

Present law. Premature withdrawals from an IRA before the beneficiary dies, becomes disabled, or attains age 59½, are subject to a penalty tax of 10%.

GUIDE TO TAX REFORM PROPOSALS 149

Proposal. Increase the penalty tax from 10% to 15%. The tax would be waived for any distribution that is part of a scheduled series of substantially level payments under an annuity for the life of the IRA owner (or the joint lives of the owner and the owner's beneficiary).

Lump-sum distributions

Present law. Lump-sum distributions from a qualified plan may qualify for special 10-year income averaging. In addition, the pre-1974 portion of any lump-sum distribution may be treated as long-term capital gain.

Proposal. Favorable 10-year averaging rules for lump-sum distributions would not be allowed to most taxpayers. In its place, a one-time election for five-year averaging would be allowed for persons age 59½ and over. If you are under age 59½ you would be allowed the election only if you reached age 50 before January 1, 1986.

If you were separated from service during December 1985 and received a lump-sum distribution in January 1986, you would be allowed to elect 10-year averaging under current law rules.

Capital gain treatment for pre-1974 contributions would be phased out over six years for individuals age 59½. Capital gain treatment under the six-year phaseout could also be claimed by individuals who reached age 50 before 1986.

Recovery of pension cost contributions

Present rule. Distributions received before the annuity starting date are treated as follows: First from nontaxable employee contributions. Second from taxable amounts allocated to employer contributions and income. Distributions after the annuity starting date are generally treated as part income and part recovery of employee contributions. If you are to receive all of your contributions within the first three years after the annuity starting date, no part of the distributions are subject to tax until you receive back all of your cost contributions.

Proposal. Reverse the tax order for distributions before the annuity starting date. Distributions would be taxable as follows: First from taxable employer contributions and income. Second from nontaxable employee contributions. This proposal would be generally effective for distributions made after December 31, 1985, but would not apply to benefits accrued prior to January 1, 1986.

Repeal the three-year recovery rule. You would treat distributions received during the year as part taxable income and part nontaxable basis recovery. The rule would not apply if the annuity starting date is on or before July 1, 1986.

When retirement benefits must be received

Present law. Generally, you must start to take benefits by April 1 of the calendar year following the year in which you reach age 70½ unless you continue working, in which case benefits must begin by April 1st following the year of retirement. However, if you are a five-percent owner, you start to take benefits by April 1st following the year you reach 70½, whether or not you retire.

Distributions from an IRA must begin no later than April 1st of the calendar year following the year in which you reach age 70½.

Proposal. Fix a uniform starting date for benefits under all qualified plans, IRAs, and tax-sheltered annuities. Distributions would be required to commence no later than April 1st of the calendar year following the year in which you reach age 70½. You could no longer defer the receipt of benefits from a qualified plan by continuing to work.

Failure to satisfy the minimum distribution rules would trigger a nondeductible excise tax of 50% on the excess of the required minimum distribution over the actual distribution.

The proposal would generally apply for distributions made after December 31, 1985. However, employees who are not five percent owners and who have attained age 70½ by January 1, 1988, may defer benefit payments until retirement.

Withdrawals before age 59½

Present law. A 10% penalty is imposed on IRA withdrawals before age 59½, unless made because of death or disability. A similar penalty applies to early withdrawals from qualified plans by five percent owners.

Proposal. Increase the penalty to 15% for all premature withdrawals from qualified plans, qualified annuity plans, and IRAs. An exception would apply to distributions that are part of a scheduled series of level payments under an annuity for the life of the participant (or the joint lives of the owner and the owner's beneficiary).

Loans from qualified plans

Present law. A qualified plan may make loans to an employee without adverse tax consequences if the loan is repayable within five years and when added to other outstanding loans from the plan does not exceed the lower of (1) $50,000 or (2) one-half of the present value of vested benefits or $10,000, whichever is greater. Further, if a loan is used to buy, build or rehabilitate a principal residence (or relative's residence), a loan within the $50,000/$10,000 limitation is not treated as a taxable distribution, even if repayable over a period of more than five years.

The loan must specifically require payment within five years or less. If not, the loan is a taxable distribution, even if repaid within five years.

Proposal. Reduce the $50,000 limit to the highest outstanding loan balance of the prior 12 months.

Allow an exception to the five-year repayment rule only for loans applied to the first-time purchase of the participant's principal residence. Level amortization of the loan over the permissible repayment period would be required.

Deny a deduction for interest on loans from 401(k) and 403(b) plans and increase the participant's basis under the plan by the amount of nondeductible interest paid.

Deferred annuity contracts

Present law. Income earned under a deferred annuity contract is taxed when paid to the policyholder. Amounts distributed before the policyholder attains age 59½ are subject to an additional 5% income tax.

The penalty tax does not apply if the distribution is one of a series of periodic payments lasting at least 60 months.

Proposal. Tax any increase in the cash surrender value of the deferred annuity contract over the basis of the contract. The owner of a deferred variable annuity contract would be treated as owning a pro-rata share of the assets and income of any separate account underlying the variable contract. As a result, the owner would not be taxed on the unrealized appreciation of assets underlying a variable contract.

The additional income tax on amounts withdrawn from deferred annuity contracts before age 59½ would be 15%.

Ceiling for qualified cash or deferred (Section 401(k)) plans

Present law. Up to the lower of $30,000 or 25% of compensation may be put into a deferral pay plan.

Proposal. Substantially reduce the tax savings available to deferral pay plans by placing a contribution ceiling of $7,000 on pay deferrals and reduce the total contribution limit from $30,000 to $25,000. Further, the IRA deduction limit would be reduced by one dollar for each dollar you contribute to a 401(k) plan. For example, if you contributed $1,500 to a 401(k) plan, you would be allowed an IRA deduction of only $500. The additional $250 spousal IRA deduction would not be reduced.

Elective deferrals and qualifying employer matching contributions to a 401(k) plan would not be permitted in years in which the employer does not have current or accumulated profits.

Nondiscrimination rules for 401(k) plan

Present law. The average of deferrals as a percent of compensation for the highest paid eligible employees (⅓) may not exceed 150% of the actual deferral percentage of the lowest paid two-thirds of eligible employees. Alternatively, the actual deferral percentage of the top one-third may not exceed the lesser of 250% of the actual deferral percent of the lowest two-thirds of employees, or the actual deferral percentage of the lowest two-thirds of employees plus three percentage points.

Proposal. The deferral percentage by an employer's highly compensated employees could not exceed 125% of the deferral percentage of eligible nonhighly compensated employees. Alternatively, the deferral percentage of an employer's highly compensated employees could not exceed the lesser of 200% of the deferral percentage of the nonhighly compensated employees, or the actual deferral percentage of the nonhighly compensated employees plus two percentage points.

An employee would be treated as highly compensated for a plan year if during the current plan year or either of the two preceding plan years he or she was:
1. A 5% owner;
2. One of the 10 employees owning the largest interest in the employer who has pay in excess of the limit on annual additions under a defined contribution plan ($25,000 for 1986).
3. An employee earning more than $50,000; or
4. One of the top 10% of employees by pay, excluding employees who earn less than $20,000, and employees who earn less than $35,000 and are not among the top 5% by compensation.

Overall limits on contributions and benefits

Defined contribution plans. The dollar limit on annual additions to a defined contribution plan would be reduced from $30,000 to $25,000.

Defined benefit plans. The dollar limit would be reduced from $90,000 to $77,000. The current $200,000 pay limit for top-heavy plans would be reduced to reflect the changes in the dollar limits.

The proposed $77,000 limit would be actuarially reduced for benefits commencing prior to age 62; but the dollar limit applicable to benefits at or after age 55 generally would not be reduced to an amount less than $65,000 (for police and firefighters, $50,000 regardless of age). In addition, the dollar limit on benefits payable to airline pilots would be reduced only if benefits commence prior to age 60.

Cost-of-living adjustments. Beginning in 1988, indexing would adjust the defined benefit plan dollar limit to reflect post-1986 cost-of-living increases. No adjustments would be made to the defined contribution plan limit until the limit equals 25% of the defined benefit plan limit. Thereafter, the defined contribution plan limit would be increased to the extent necessary to maintain the limit equal to 25% of the defined benefit plan limit.

Employees could make additional contributions to a qualified cost-of-living account under a pension plan, to provide post-retirement cost-of-living increases.

Combined plan limit. Under present law, a combined plan limit applies to an individual who participates in both a defined contribution plan and a defined benefit pension plan of the same employer. The combined plan limit would be retained.

Tax on excess distributions. A 15% excise tax would be imposed on aggregate annual distributions from all tax-favored retirement arrangements in excess of the greater of $112,500 or 1.25 times the defined benefit plan dollar limit.

Contributions to pension and other plans

Present law. Annual employer contributions are generally limited to the greater of the amount needed to satisfy the minimum funding requirements of the pension plan or 25% of the aggregate compensation of covered employees. This limit does not apply when an employee participates in both a defined benefit and money-purchase pension plan of the same employer.

Proposal. If an employee participates in both a defined benefit and money-purchase pension plan then the employer's deduction generally would be limited to the greater of (1) the amount needed to satisfy the minimum funding requirements of the defined benefit pension plan or (2) 25% of the aggregate compensation of covered employees.

Carryforward of profit-sharing and stock-bonus plans contributions

Present law. Employer contributions to a profit-sharing or stock-bonus plan are deductible in the year paid up to 15% of aggregate compensation. If an annual contribution is less than the deduction limit, the unused amount may be carried over to a later year.

Proposal. Employer contributions would be deductible in the year paid to the extent that the contributions when added to the employer's share of Social Security taxes taken into account, under the plan (if any) did not exceed 15% of aggregate compensation.
Repeal the limit carryforward for all profit-sharing and stock-bonus plans.

Voluntary matching contributions

Present law. If employer contributions are conditioned on an employee's contributions, the employer's matching contributions must be nondiscriminatory.

Proposal. Place various percentage limitations on total voluntary employee contributions and employer matching contributions.
Contributions to highly paid employees exceeding the amount permitted under the matching contribution rules would be deductible but subject to a 10% excise tax, unless the excess, plus earnings were distributed in a timely manner.

156 IRA, KEOGH, AND OTHER RETIREMENT PLANS

Nondiscrimination rules for qualified plans

Present law. A qualified plan generally must meet either a percentage test, or a "fair cross section" test. A plan meets the percentage test by covering at least 70% of all employees; or, if at least 70% of all employees are eligible to participate, the plan benefits 80% of those participants. A plan meets the "fair cross section" test if the Treasury determines that the classification of covered employees does not discriminate in favor of employees who are officers, shareholders, or highly compensated.

Proposal. The Treasury should study the effect of the present law coverage tests, and recommend new coverage rules. The study and recommendations must be submitted to Congress no later than July 1, 1986.

Nondiscrimination rule for defined benefit plans

Present law. A plan meets the nondiscrimination rules if benefits provided under the plan bear a uniform relationship to compensation. To test whether benefits bear a uniform relationship to compensation, the employer-provided share of an employee's Social Security benefit may be considered. Under certain circumstances, Social Security benefits earned with a prior employer may also be considered.

Proposal. Benefits earned with a prior employer could not be considered. Qualified plans would be required to comply with this requirement for plan years beginning after December 31, 1985. Plan amendments containing this provision would not be required until plan years beginning on or after January 1, 1988.

Top-heavy plans

Present law. A plan is top-heavy if more than 60% of the value of cumulative accrued benefits are provided for key employees. No uniform accrual rule is provided for testing whether a plan is top-heavy.

Proposal. A uniform benefit accrual rule would be applied in testing whether a defined benefit plan is top-heavy. A fractional benefit accrual rule of present law would apply solely to determine whether a plan is top-heavy or super top-heavy. The proposal would be effective for plan years beginning after December 31, 1985.

Deferral plans of state and local government and tax-exempt employers (Section 457 plans)

Present law. An employee may elect annual deferrals equal to the lesser of $7,500 or 33⅓% of compensation (net of the deferral). The participant is taxed on the distribution of the deferred amounts.

Proposal. Distributions would be required to satisfy a payout schedule under which benefits projected to be paid over the lifetime of the participant are at least 66⅔% of the total benefits payable.

Distributions must be paid on a substantially nonincreasing basis. After the death of the employee, payment of benefits to the employee's beneficiary must begin within one year after the employee's death. Certain tax-free rollovers between deferred compensation plans would be permitted.

Asset reversions under qualified plans

Present law. Assets remaining in a qualified defined benefit pension plan generally may be paid to the employer after plan benefits accrued to the date of plan termination have been provided. Assets reverted to an employer are includible in the employer's gross income.

Proposal. Assets reverting to an employer pursuant to a plan termination occurring after December 31, 1985 would be subject to a nondeductible excise tax equal to 10% of the amount reverted.

Nondeductible contributions

Present law. Employer contributions in excess of the deduction limit may be carried over and deducted in later years.

Proposal. Impose a 15% annual nondeductible excise tax on employer contributions in excess of the deductible limits until the excess is eliminated.

Benefit forfeitures

Present law. Forfeitures in a money-purchase pension plan must be used to reduce future employer contributions or to offset plan administrative expenses.

Proposal. Reallocate forfeitures to remaining participants. The proposal would be effective for plan years ending after December 31, 1985.

The J. K. Lasser Tax Institute carries on the tax, financial, and business publications of J. K. Lasser. The Institute, under the direction of Bernard Greisman, continues the J. K. Lasser tradition of explaining complicated and technical material in terms understandable by the layman. It is also noted for its special tax services for professionals. The most widely read work for the public by the Institute is J. K. Lasser's Your Income Tax which has helped over 28 million taxpayers reduce taxes and make informed financial decisions.

West Hills College Coalinga
Fitch Library
300 Cherry Lane
Coalinga, CA 93210